Keep Alma #1! Live
'em Outrageous
Service!

Ordering Information

This book is also available on cassette!
If you would like to order more books or cassettes,
please contact Tiger Books, Inc.
at 501-801-2665 (BOOK)
or 1-800-946-2666,

write to:
Tiger Books, Inc.
Post Office Box 3525
Little Rock, AR 72203-3525,

visit our website at www.tigerbooks.net,

or complete the order form on the reverse of this page

Outrageous Money Back Guarantee!

We are so convinced that this book will help you
and your company have more satisfied customers,
satisfied employees, and profitable results that
we will give you your money back if not totally
satisfied within 90 days of the purchase date.
(Limit one book per customer)
Simply send your book back to:

Greg Hatcher
The Hatcher Agency
P.O. Box 3505, Little Rock, AR 72203.

TIGER

Books, Inc.

"There is No Off Switch on a Tiger"

Order Form for *55 Steps to Outrageous Service*
by Greg Hatcher

Name _____

Shipping Address _____

_____

Phone _____ Fax _____

E-mail _____

Outrageous Money Back Guarantee!
We are so convinced that this book will help you and your company have more satisfied customers, satisfied employees, and profitable results that we will give you your money back if not totally satisfied within 90 days of the purchase date. Simply send your book back to: Greg Hatcher, The Hatcher Agency, P. O. Box 3505, Little Rock, AR 72203

Item	Quantity	Cost Per Item	Total Cost
Outrageous Service **Book**		$29.95	
Outrageous Service **Cassette**		$39.95	
Outrageous Service **Book /Tape Set**		$59.95	
Shipping & Handling (Book/Tape Set Counts as 2 Items)		$3.50	
Subtotal			
Sales Tax		.06125	
Total			

Payment Type ☐ Check ☐ Charge ☐ Cash

Credit Card # _____ Expiration Date _____

Type ☐ Visa ☐ MasterCard ☐ American Express ☐ Discover

Signature _____ Date _____

You may fax this order form to **501-801-3554** or mail to:

Tiger Books, Inc.
P.O. Box 3525
Little Rock, AR 72203
Phone: 501-801-2665 (BOOK) or 1-800-946-2666

ORDER TAKEN BY   Sales Code: 001

55 STEPS TO
OUTRAGEOUS SERVICE

GREG HATCHER
CLU, CHC,ChFC, RHU, REBC

Tiger Books, Inc.
Little Rock, AR

For information, contact
Tiger Books, Inc.
P.O. Box 3525
Little Rock, AR 72203
501-801-2665 or 1-800-946-2666

I dedicate this book to my wife, Lee;
my four children, Kelsey, Haley, Larkin, and Layne;
my parents, Joe and Irma Gail Hatcher;
my brother, Geoff; my sister, Gailyn;
and my father-in-law and mother-in-law,
Dr. Bill and Sandra Tranum.
Thanks to all of you for always being there with all the
help you gave me to build The Hatcher Agency.

Acknowledgments

I would like to give special thanks to the many people who have helped influence my life and helped me develop the "Outrageous Service" concepts outlined in this book.

To Morley Fraser, the former football and baseball coach at Albion College, for his initial teaching advice that we always work 24 hours a day to take care of the customer;

to Zig Ziglar for his inspirational tapes and books that have kept me working and inspired for years;

to John Russ, my personal coach, who has told me on countless occasions that I had more than one book in me;

to Larry Waschka, author of *The Complete Idiot's Guide To Getting Rich*, who helped inspire me to write this book and has been a business colleague with whom I have shared ideas for many years;

to Curtis Bailey, my good friend and co-worker, who has always been there to help me get through anything from moving my furniture to listening to me as I got through crises;

to Joyce White who typed this entire book from my numerous dictation tapes;

to Jamie Harrison, my friend since childhood, who has always stood rock solid beside me;

to Scott Allison, my friend and former co-worker who always has an optimistic outlook no matter how tough a foe he may be facing and who always makes insurance fun while still being focused;

to Don Roescheise, a 60-year-old millionaire, who has been my cheerleader from the day I started the company and has rooted us on to success all along the way, while not taking a drink in 12 years and counting, while living his life one day at a time;

to my father- and mother-in-law, Bill and Sandra Tranum, who have been excellent role models for me and my wife;

to Doug Fraser, the former football coach at Birmingham-Seaholm High School, who has a single-minded focus for success like no one I have ever known;

to Jim Foley, a Manager for Unum Life Insurance Company, whose drive and competitiveness have helped me continue to be inspired in my business and personal life;

to Nancy Russ, for her tireless and quick work in editing this book;

to Jim Lewis of Corporate Benefit Solutions who believed in us from the start and has always given us outrageous service;

to Tom Peters for all the tapes and books that have continued to enhance my motivational education;

to Eugene Pattison, my college English professor and fraternity advisor, for his support 20 plus years and counting;

to Bruce Dickey and Bill Klenk, my college soccer, wrestling, and baseball coaches, who taught me how to pay the price for success, and that you can be a winner without winning the game;

to Rudy Pollan, a business friend who volunteered two months of his time to help build our agency for no pay;

to my wife, Lee, for her support and hours spent helping me improve The Hatcher Agency;

to my mother, Irma Gail Hatcher, for the time she donated in the early years and for her zest to be the best;

and most of all to my father, Joe Hatcher, whose honesty and straightforwardness in business naturally ingrained in me over the years a business sense as natural to me as hitting a homerun is for Ken Griffey, Jr.

I used to think that the things that were obvious to me in business should be obvious to everyone, but I did not realize until later that the difference was that everyone was not raised by my father.

Thank You

A special thank you to some of the very best insurance professionals and friends I have had the pleasure to work with. They are all "All Stars" in their specialties and they have helped us build our agency.

1. Corporate Benefit Solutions – Jim Lewis, Bob Bracy, Bob Bridwell, and Vivian Joiner
2. Spradley & Coker – Jim Spradley and Daryl Coker
3. Unum Life – Jim Foley, Tom Coyne, and Brian Dillion
4. Delta Dental – Earl Gladden and Cheryl Lewis
5. Prudential – Charles Carter and Brian Forbes
6. Agency Services – Jiggs Ramsey and Don Mowrey
7. Penn Mutual – Tony Fakouri and Curt Spelzhaus
8. American Heritage Life – David Bird and Bryan Kelly
9. Blue Cross Blue Shield – Dr. George Mitchell, Jim Bailey, Steve Spaulding, Bob Shoptaw, Sharon Allen, Bill Phillips, Mike Brown, Rick Hammil, Ron DeBerry, John Greer, Kenny Lewis, Dee Rodgers, Johnny Runnells, and Deborah Wyatt
10. Meadors & Adams – Andrew Meadors
11. Stephens Insurance – Bobby Whitfield
12. The Honea Agency – Ross Honea
13. Pharmacy Associates, Inc. – Robert Bumpas and Terry Baskin
14. Old Northwest Agents – Peter Zornik
15. Delta Dental – Eddie Choate and Robert Bumpas
16. USAble Life – Jim House, Julie Marshall, Max Kane, and Dave Henderson
17. QualChoice – Frances Browning, Paula Wilbanks, and Roy Lamm
18. Flexco, Inc. – Barry Roe
19. Allison Financial Services – Scott Allison
20. Novasys – Robin Reeves
21. The Grace Agency – Ted Grace and Rick Angel
22. Crews & Associates – Rush Harding
23. Trent Capital Management – David Trent
24. Lax, Vaughn, Evans & Fortson – Mike Lax

A Special Thank You to The Hatcher Agency Staff

Front Row (L-R): Robert Ellis, Wendy Ivy, Dawn Anders, Lori Baker, Charla Reynolds, Leah Kirkland, Trish Blaylock, Dottie Highfill, and Curtis Bailey.

Back Row (L-R): Adam May, Woody Harrelson, Jackie DeMott, Pat Winbury, Joyce White, Greg Hatcher, Paige White, Linda Pitts, Celia Haas, Iley "Junior" Ward, Blake Byars, and Matt Dalton.

Without your hard work and dedication to "Outrageous Service," we would not be writing this book.

Contents

P A R T   T H R E E

"Outrageous Service" Ideas

Some Assumptions

I certainly don't want to offend anyone when telling some of my stories and using examples throughout this book. I have referred to the third person as "he" rather than "he or she" or "him or her" for simplicity's sake, but I want everyone to read the book as if it could apply to a man or a woman.

PART ONE

"Outrageous Service" Philosophies

Just Win the Damn Ballgame!

I began learning the principles of Outrageous Service in my first job after high school graduation. Along with three other college students, I was hired to work for the summer for Morley Fraser, who was head football and baseball coach for Albion College and one of the greatest motivators of all time. Morley was the kind of fiery coach that books are written and movies are made about.

But Morley never made it to "the big time" because he chose to stay at an NCAA Division III school in Michigan. He and his wife had three sons and two daughters, and Morley passed up many offers to coach Division I and II schools. He chose to stay in this small Michigan town where he had the time to see his kids play sports and where he could coach his own athletes. Each of his three sons quarterbacked the high school football team. One was killed in a car wreck after high school, and the other two went on to play in college and become head football coaches. The girls were also athletes, and both married coaches. It is an understatement to say that the Fraser family was competitive.

During the summer, Morley served as Director of Continuing Education for Albion College. The program included approximately 40 different camps and conferences that ranged from cheerleading camps to IBM business conferences, and from church groups to every sport imaginable.

Morley's "Big Four," as we were called, were on call 24 hours a day, and our job description was to do whatever it took to keep the campers and staff happy. The ultimate goal was to ensure that every contract would be renewed for the next summer.

The Big Four, all under age 22, were armed with master keys to the college campus. Our primary responsibility was to plan the leisure and sports activities. But, we were also responsible for seeing that conference rooms were set up, the residential rooms were clean, the laundry was picked up and any other task that affected the campers' satisfaction.

We often had as many as four conferences in the same week. At the beginning of each conference, Morley called us in to outline the game plan and assign responsibilities to each of the Big Four. The duties were broad, but the mission was simple: "Do whatever it takes to make these campers happy and Win the Damn Ballgame."

As a football coach, Morley knew that there are many ways to win a football game. You can pass; you can run; you can play great defense; you can have great special teams play; you can make wonderful play calls. But Morley also knew that all that matters when the game is over is who has the winning score. He didn't care what method we chose as long as we played by the rules and won.

Morley often told us that each of us had a different set of skills, and we were to utilize those skills to make the customers happy. We took little old ladies to church; we took men's groups to taverns; sometimes we rushed people to the airport; other times we went to the local diner to get special food for someone or to the drug store to get a prescription filled. There was no job too big or too small for us to do, and any hour of the day or night was "convenient" for us.

I remember picking up hundreds of bags of dirty linen from the dormitories and loading them on the linen truck in 85-degree heat. The smell was unbelievable.

I also remember getting to have a few beers with the instructors from the cheerleading camps. This was quite a treat for a 19-year-old boy.

In the first couple of years with Morley, I would go into his office and ask a question about what to do about some problem at one of the conferences. Sometimes he would give me suggestions and help me decide what to do. However, if I brought him a problem he thought I could solve on my own, he would simply look me in the eye and say, "Hatcher, get out of my office and win the damn ballgame." It was a unique style of coaching and development, but a very effective one that I have incorporated in my business. In almost all situations, employees can figure out how to solve the problems if we will allow them to use their initiative.

I was not always the brightest or the most talented member of Morley's Big Four, but I will never forget what he told me when I left after working for him for four summers. He said that I did not always do things exactly the way he would do them, but that he had never had anyone work for him who was as good at figuring out a way to win the ballgame. That was high praise coming from Morley Fraser.

The most important thing I learned from Morley and Albion College was that good customer service is an attitude. Fraser taught me that every detail is important and no detail is too big or too small to take care of if it helps win the ballgame. The coach helped me develop the ability to probe, ask questions, listen to people and figure out what they want—and then go get it for them. That was the beginning of my concept of Outrageous Service.

"Outrageous Service:" service that is
so above and beyond the ordinary
that people will talk about it.

CHAPTER

The Definition of "Outrageous Service"

In order to understand the above definition, let's look first at service that is not outrageous.

You go into a burger joint and order a burger with pickles and lettuce only. When you get your burger, it has pickles and lettuce, and ketchup and mustard. When you complain, the clerk takes the burger and gives you what you ordered, a burger with pickles and lettuce only. That is service—but it is not Outrageous Service. It is what you expect when you don't get what you ordered. You're not likely to go back to the office and tell your coworkers about the incident. If the burger joint practiced Outrageous Service, the clerk would replace your hamburger with what you ordered and tell you there would be no charge for it. Or, perhaps you would get a gift certificate for two free hamburgers. More than likely you would tell other people about the Outrageous Service you received. Everybody makes mistakes, but some mistakes can become marketing tools.

Examples of what "Outrageous Service" *is* happens on a daily basis at the Hatcher Agency. A customer calls the agency and asks for a supply of claim forms. The customer expects us to mail the forms to be received in a couple of days. Our customer service representative says, "We will be happy to get you some extra claim forms," and a courier is dispatched to deliver the forms, along with a bag of gourmet cookies, that afternoon.

The receptionist who takes a call when an employee is out and offers to give the customer the car phone and home number of the employee is going the second mile. But, when that receptionist calls the employee's car or phone number so the employee can return the call immediately, the customer is impressed. If a company demonstrates this kind of attentiveness on a regular basis, that is "Outrageous Service."

Service is only outrageous when it is part of company policy. The CEO or any other executive in a company cannot deliver "Outrageous Service" unless every employee understands the concept and practices it consistently.

It takes a lot of pumping to get
a well to produce water;
but once you get water, all you have
to do is pump gently and you'll have
all the water you ever wanted.

3

The History of
The Hatcher Agency

"The Home of Outrageous Service" started September 1, 1990

In September 1990, I hired a secretary and took a three-year lease on 500 square feet of office space. I had a simple mission: to provide the most "Outrageous Service" in the insurance industry. Four months later, we hired two more employees and added more space. By the end of one year, we had seven employees.

Three years later the Hatcher Agency was the state's largest health insurance agency and was named Arkansas' Small Business of the Year by *Arkansas Business* newsmagazine.

Today we have 23 full time employees. For more than eight years, we have continued to grow, in spite of the fact that we do very little prospecting for new clients and we don't advertise in print or electronic media. Nearly 100 percent of our clients come to us by referral from other clients, friends and business associates. Our advertising comes from satisfied customers who are so impressed with our "Outrageous Service" that they tell other people about us.

I majored in public relations and advertising in college, and nobody believes in advertising more than I do. However, we have elected to spend our advertising budget on our customers rather than in the media.

Sometimes we use our advertising dollars to pay better salaries so we can get the most capable employees. We know that employees who are rewarded for their service are happier employees, and we know that happy employees provide better service to their customers. We hire the best employees we can find; we expect them to offer outrageous service; and we compensate them well for their efforts.

The money most companies would allocate for advertising may be used to provide more training for employees so they know how to better serve customers. Every employee in our office is required to pass the insurance exam and become licensed. We believe that people who understand our customers' business can offer better service. Training is ongoing because none of us ever knows all there is to know about the insurance business.

A big part of our advertising budget is also spent on our customers. If we make a mistake, we not only spend whatever it takes to rectify the error, but we often do something special for the customer to make up for the error. We also give our customers T-shirts and other advertising specialties as daily reminders that we care about them and their business. In any business, the best way to advertise is to take such good care of your clients that they will talk about you to other business people. A reputation for outrageous service is the best advertisement you can have.

I am certainly aware that advertising in the print and electronic media can bring increased business. At this point in our business I have not wanted to grow too fast. We have consistently averaged a 30 percent growth each year, and I am comfortable with that. If we advertised for new customers, we could possibly bring in customers at a faster rate; but at the Hatcher Agency, we are not interested in one-time customers. Faster growth could limit our ability to deliver outrageous service. It is essential that we have top quality staff who are trained and capable of delivering that service when we get new customers.

As the Hatcher Agency approaches its ninth birthday, it is the largest health insurance agency in the state of Arkansas. For seven consecutive years, the National Association of Health Underwriters has named us as one of the top 12 producers in the United States. These numbers are astounding for a producer in a city the size of Little Rock with a population of 250,000.

The formula for success in business is fairly simple: Sell the best product and provide the best service. That's like saying the formula for staying in shape physically is simple: Exercise and eat right. In both cases, the trick is having the discipline to stick to the formula.

Discipline at the Hatcher Agency means 7:00 a.m. staff meetings and 7:00 to 6:00 working hours. For every employee it means studying and passing the insurance exam. It means being willing to shift gears and do whatever it takes to handle a problem. This kind of discipline separates the Hatcher Agency from most businesses in America.

The secret to success is simple. The key to implementing it is very difficult. It requires Discipline, Discipline, Discipline.

CHAPTER

Outrageous
Work Hours
(24 Hours a Day, of Course)

Our work hours at The Hatcher Agency are the same as mine were when I worked the summer camps at Albion College—24 hours a day. The Agency officially opens at 7:00 a.m. and closes at 6:00 p.m. Monday through Friday. However, we have an answering service with a live person that answers the phone 24 hours a day for matters that need immediate attention.

When our answering service answers the phone for us after hours, the caller hears, "The Hatcher Agency 24 hour message center. How can I help you?" If a customer needs to talk to someone or has a problem with his health insurance coverage, the person answering the phone offers our home phone numbers, pager numbers, and car phone numbers without ever asking for a name. There is nothing more infuriating than to call a company and ask for someone's car phone number and hear, "May I ask who is calling?" before you are given a number.

We want our customers to know that home phone numbers, pager numbers, and car phone numbers are always available to them. If someone has a problem he feels cannot wait until tomorrow, we might as well fix it now and make the caller happy. We are going to have to fix it sooner or later anyway.

Each sales and service representative that works with our clients is furnished a pager and a car phone paid in full by The Hatcher Agency. When we interview candidates, we let them know right off the bat that if they are going to work for us, they are going to have to be committed to servicing the customer. This may include an occasional phone call at home and the necessity that they carry a pager and have a car phone. We want to scare off in the initial interviewing process any prospective employee that is the least bit intimidated about this because we only hire employees who will deliver "Outrageous Service." Actually, I don't get many phone calls at home or pages after hours; but when I do, it feels wonderful to be able to deliver service that is extraordinary and is above and beyond the call of duty.

What is interesting is that my employees and I get more satisfaction out of helping a person after hours than during business hours because the opportunity does not come often and it is almost always well received.

Car phone numbers, pagers, home phone and our 800 number are printed on business cards so when a customer calls us, it's on our dime. The very fact that we are willing to give them access to us 24 hours a day tells our customers a whole lot about the type of service they are going to receive.

Tell People What You Are Going To Do, and Then Do It

(It ain't braggin' if you can back it up.)

Do you remember the night in 1969 when the New York Jets won the Super Bowl? Up to that time the NFC had dominated football, and the Green Bay Packers had won the first two Super Bowls. But this year the Jets, representing the AFC, were facing the Baltimore Colts in Super Bowl III. The Jets—considered a major underdog in the contest—had a flamboyant, almost outrageous quarterback named Joe Namath. Joe boldly announced to the media that the Jets would beat the Colts in the Super Bowl, and he guaranteed a victory. The brash quarterback and his boisterous promise got a lot of coverage in the media. By the time the game started, Joe Namath's reputation was on the line.

When the game was over, the New York Jets were the winners. Joe had lived up to his boast. Anyone who has ever seen highlights of the previous Super Bowls will remember the clip of Joe Namath walking off the field raising his hands in the air with his index finger held high, waving to the crowd that the New York Jets were Number One.

Why is this story significant to the understanding of "Outrageous Service?" Because Joe Namath practiced the kind of advertising that leads to a successful company.

There are two ways to deliver "Outrageous Service." One way is by consistently doing great and wonderful things for your customer, allowing the customer to slowly but surely notice that you are delivering services beyond their expectations. The problem with this strategy is that it may take six months, a year, or even ten years for the public to notice the "Outrageous Service" your organization is providing.

The other way to deliver this "Outrageous Service" is the Joe Namath approach. Tell your customers you are going to be open at 7:00 a.m. and will answer their calls immediately, that you will be available by car phone or home phone when they need you, that your product will be stronger and your service better than any other vendor they have used. Then back up your claims of "Outrageous Service" by doing what you said you would do and more. The customer will notice your "Outrageous Service" immediately. Perhaps even more importantly, customers will be so impressed that they will tell other people about you. What sounded like bragging becomes advertising. "It ain't bragging if you can back it up!"

Imagine what would happen if Burger King or McDonald's ran a television ad that claimed "McDonald's is a great place to go for hamburgers," and never mentioned their fast service?

What if TCBY didn't advertise the fact that their desserts are healthy, or if Federal Express never mentioned that they turn packages around quickly? The key to having people notice your business and seek out your services—and to having them tell others about your services—is to get the word out about the kind of service you will deliver. Then when you back up your promises with great delivery and a few extra special service surprises, that puts the icing on the cake.

Some business people believe that the key to success is to deliver more than is expected. I believe that if in the selling process you teach the customer not to expect much from you, you may never get the chance to show them your services. People tend not to buy services or products if they don't expect to get much in return. It is true that the customer may get used to your "Outrageous Service" and consider it routine. But customers who leave you will be reminded very quickly of what they are missing, and they won't be long in coming back to you.

Tell people what you are going to do for them and then do it. As Joe Namath proved, "It ain't braggin' if you can do it."

CHAPTER

On Your Worst Day You Must Still Be Very Good

In sales and customer service, on your worst day you must still be very good.

Customers operate on the principle of "What have you done for me lately?" You can take care of a customer for years and then fail to deliver what he wants just once and put that account in jeopardy. This is the flip side of "Outrageous Service." One bad experience can negate years of extraordinary service.

Think about it in your own life. Have you ever had a bad experience in a store where you had done business for years? Someone was short with you, didn't treat you right, or had a poor attitude toward you? You may have made a decision never to go in that store again. Furthermore, you may have told your friends about your experience, causing them to think twice before doing business with that store.

The bottom line is that a company simply cannot afford "bad days" that affect customer service. Regardless of how bad the employee feels or how many things have gone wrong, the employee must remember that every contact with the customer is crucial. One failure to render good service could mean the loss of that account.

Customers who get the kind of service they expect from a business are not likely to talk about it. A customer who is irate, or even slightly annoyed, with the service is almost certain to tell someone. People talk loudly and passionately when their emotions are involved. If our customers are going to be excited, we want them to be excited about the "outrageously positive" service we've delivered.

It takes a super-special effort to get customers to take the time and make the effort to tell others about the service they received from our company. The great news is that the extra effort it takes to make customers happy also makes employees feel good. And, it is a lot more effective and less expensive way to get new customers than advertising on the radio, in the newspapers or on TV.

Be very good on your worst days, and you will get free advertising. Your customers will be walking billboards for you.

CHAPTER

7

The Hatcher Agency Employee Job Description

Listed below is The Hatcher Agency's job description for all employees:

That is part of the job description of every employee at the Hatcher Agency. It means what it says. The employee has the authority to do whatever it takes to provide 100 percent satisfaction for the customer.

When people see this statement on the bronze plaque in the agency's employee training room, they often ask, "Does that mean what it says?" Yes. "You mean employees can spend money when they feel it is merited without consulting the boss?" Yes. "What if your employee makes a decision to give away thousands of dollars to a customer?" Most people—including business owners—are amazed that I would give employees that kind of freedom.

Actually, that policy is a major key to the "Outrageous Service" the agency offers. Suppose a customer who is unhappy comes in. The employee knows what to do to fix the problem, but it involves spending money or leaving the office for a few hours to fix the problem. I may be in a meeting outside the office or on an airplane. Our customers are busy people. They don't have time to sit and wait while an employee tracks down someone who can give him or her the authority to take the action needed.

The employee may make a decision to give away some company dollars to fix the problem. He may give away too much money or do something I would have considered absurd, but it pleases the customer. My only problem is that the employee spent a little too much money. That is a minor problem when weighed against the good news that we have a very satisfied customer. It is easy to train the employee on how to make the customer satisfied without spending so much money the next time. Winning back a customer who leaves because the employee does not have the freedom to do what is needed is more difficult.

An even bigger problem is that unsatisfied customers generally tell an average of five people when they receive unsatisfactory service, so I've not only lost that customer, I may have lost five other potential accounts. The employee who spent a little too much money but provided Outrageous Service has boosted our advertising.

I heard a story that illustrates my point about employee authority.

A well-known grocery store chain was outstanding at giving its employees latitude in making sure the customer was happy. A lady walked into the store after Thanksgiving passing a 17-year-old clerk at the checkout stand.

The clerk said, "How are you doing Ma'am?"

"Not very good at all," she said. "My Thanksgiving turkey was really dry and it did not taste very good."

"I'm sorry," the young man said. "Please come over to my register." He ripped off a sheet of paper and wrote on it: "One Free Turkey." He gave it to the lady and told her to go back to the meat department for her free turkey. She thanked him and headed for the meat department.

A reporter who was standing in the checkout line just could not believe that this 17-year-old kid was allowed to give away a turkey without first consulting a manager.

He said, "You just gave that lady a free turkey without even asking any questions. She could have overcooked the turkey, or she may just be a complainer."

The clerk said, "The owner of this store wants us to have satisfied customers."

"But a turkey is quite an expensive item to be giving away free," the reporter argued.

The boy answered "Yeah, I guess so. A turkey costs about $35."

The reporter persisted, "What is a typical purchase here at the grocery store?" The clerk told him it was "about $100 a week." The reporter said, "Gosh, $35 on a $100 order is a 35 percent loss."

"That is one way to look at it," the boy responded. "But the way I look at it is that the average customer spends $100 a week in the store and comes in our store 50 weeks a year. If you take 50 weeks times $100, you have $5,000 in grocery revenue. Our average customer lives in this area approximately 10 years, which works out to $5,000 times 10 years, or $50,000. Furthermore, that lady will leave the store and tell at least five of her friends how this store backs up its products and service. I just spent $35 to keep $300,000 (the $50,000 customer and her 5 friends at $250,000) worth of business. That $35 may be the best advertising money the company spends this year."

"I still find it hard to believe that your boss allows you to make that decision," the reporter said.

The young man replied, "If I went to my boss and told him that I lost $300,000 in sales today because I would not give away $35, I would get fired. So you see, whether or not I made a good decision depends on how you look at things."

This young man saw the big picture. He knew that keeping customers satisfied is worth a few dollars here and there. Regardless of where the fault lies, it is the employee's responsibility to keep the customer happy. My old boss, Morley Fraser, taught me "In a disagreement, if there is even a possibility that you are 10 percent wrong, take all the responsibility." The clerk didn't need to find out whether the woman overcooked the turkey. He just needed to do something to make her happy.

The great thing about our employee job description is that it allows each employee to creatively fix whatever problem comes up in order to help the customer win the ballgame.

As I was dictating this chapter, an event occurred that provided one of my employees an opportunity to deliver outstanding customer service. We had a customer whose building burned over the weekend in a town about an hour away from our office. Our employee called their office the next morning to see if everyone was all right and to ask how long it would be before they were able to resume work in their building. We were told that they had no phone lines other than temporary mobile phones. They would be moving to a nearby warehouse building to set up temporary office quarters while they built a new location in the next few months. The employee to whom we talked explained that things were kind of rough because they did not even have a soft drink machine. They had no vending machines or any way to get a snack during the day.

Our employee, who happened to know that this particular customer preferred water to soft drinks, called a local bottling company and had a couple of cases of bottled water sent out to the account. All of this was done without management approval while I was in Columbus, Ohio, seeing an insurance carrier. I cannot tell you how good I felt to know that "Outrageous Service" was being delivered even when I was not in the office. This could only happen because our employees have the freedom to spend money to take care of the customer.

*Of all the things you wear, your
expression is the most important.*

CHAPTER

Brainwash Yourself on the Way to Work

Human beings are selfish. We spend most of our time focusing on what is best for us. Even when we do something for someone else, we generally want to know what we are going to get out of it. When most human beings go to work they do a job that is closer to the minimum that is required than the maximum effort that could be put forth. The key to having a successful organization is to find incentives to get your employees to do what is most convenient for the customer instead of what is most convenient for them.

All of us have opportunities to get by with just putting forth a minimal amount of effort and still have a fairly satisfied customer. In some cases customers may not even know that we did not do the very best thing for them. Most people take the easy route and justify it by saying that they are extremely busy, and that they are still doing a better job than most other companies. Or they may just feel like "hey, if the customer didn't bargain for it, why should I deliver it?" The key to "Outrageous Service" is to realize that each of us has a natural instinct to want to take the easy way out every now and then. When that temptation arises and we are about to succumb, we have to step up and say, "I am going to do what is convenient for the customer and offer a little extra."

To illustrate what I mean, let me give you an example that we can all relate to. You go out and have a big dinner with drinks, etc. When you come home you feel a little sluggish, and the easiest thing to do is to lie on the couch, watch a little TV and go to bed. This is the most convenient thing to do when you know the best thing you could do is get some exercise. You could put on your jogging shoes and go for a little jog, or you could do a workout. You would work off that sluggish feeling and burn a few calories. Then you would feel better and could be more productive the rest of the evening. From time to time, I find myself wanting to take the easy way and "crash." But I know that the key to overcoming that sluggish feeling is to take the first step on a jog or get into the workout room. When I do, I am always glad I did because it makes me feel so good.

Giving "Outrageous Service" by doing the little extras that are convenient for your customer and are not necessarily convenient for you will make you feel good that you have given great service. Most importantly, while customers may not recognize the absence of extra service, they will notice its presence. When you offer extra services they did not ask for and that are above and beyond the ordinary, they really get a good feeling that you are taking good care of them. Once you deliver this type of service, you will stand out because there are so few people that are willing to do the little extras. The result will be that you will get referrals on a regular basis.

Have you ever been to a mechanic to have a certain item fixed and asked him to check out a particular piece of machinery? He gives you the bill, and as you are walking out you say, "By the way, I noticed this part was not working well either." The mechanic might say "Well yeah, I thought that might be wrong too, but this is all you wanted me to fix."

You aren't likely to use that mechanic again.

By contrast, suppose you take an item to a mechanic to get it fixed. The mechanic fixes the item you ask him to fix, but lets you know there was also a problem with something else, and he took the liberty to fix that too. It was such a minor item that he fixed it at no charge. In addition, this mechanic shows you how to work the piece of machinery to prevent future problems. This type of service makes you feel very assured that you are getting great service. It is very likely that you will be back in the future. In addition, you will probably tell your friends about how good this particular mechanic is and how you can count on him to be honest and do what is best for you.

If you do what is convenient for other people instead of what is convenient for yourself, you will have more business than you can handle. However, if you take the shortcut and do not do what is most convenient for your customers, they will eventually notice and move on to another vendor.

A bronzed sign on the front of The Hatcher Agency building reads, "The Hatcher Agency was started in September 1990 with a simple mission to provide the most 'Outrageous Service' in the insurance industry." It is our goal to try to figure out ways to make insurance

more convenient for our customers instead of making things more convenient for ourselves. The reason this is on the front of the building is that I want every customer to know what our goal is and I want every employee to be reminded of our original mission statement. In the end, if you do things that are most convenient for the customer, you will reap the benefits of having more customers than you will ever need. This is a win/win situation that meets everybody's needs.

The hardest part of staying with this strategy is that it takes discipline to overcome your natural tendencies to take the easy way out. This is true whether it is watching TV versus working out after that big meal or doing a little extra for your customer when maybe you are a little busy or tired. "Outrageous Service," however, requires that you do what is most convenient for the customer instead of what is most convenient for you.

CHAPTER

There is No Off Switch on a Tiger!

This slogan has been bronzed and is in a work area that we all use on a daily basis to get the mail out and make photocopies. I am not sure where I heard this slogan the first time, but I absolutely love it. The slogan says so well what I believe about the attitude it takes to be successful in today's work environment.

The schedule I expect all our employees, including myself, to follow is walk in the door, turn on the light, and get busy.

In many offices, employees come in, get their morning cup of coffee, spend 15 to 20 minutes chatting about what happened the day before and waste the first 30 minutes of the day. Based on an eight-hour day, that is one sixteenth of the workday. These same people may spend an hour to an hour and a half lunch doing something that is totally unproductive. Finally, toward the end of the day they may spend the last 30 minutes of the day procrastinating or dreaming about what they are going to do when they get off work. Some start to gather all their things together to end the day; others end the day with another personal conversation with a fellow worker.

Obviously, we all need to be semi-sociable at work, but there are many individuals that waste more than two hours each day doing things that are unproductive. That is 25 percent of the workday!

I try to teach my staff to work hard and efficiently during work hours. Everyone on my staff knows that I love coming to work. I see work as a challenge. When I come in and turn on the lights, I get busy and do not stop until I turn the light switch off at the end of the day. This means that every hour of my day is productive. I can be quite intense about this. For instance, if I eat lunch in the office, I may be reviewing paperwork or reading an article that I need to read. Or, I may use that time for conversation with a fellow employee to see how things are going in his or her area. Sometimes I visit with a client during lunch and use the time to explore what the agency can do to improve our service. If I am on the road, I often eat in the car to save time; but I never say to myself "I have an hour lunch break and by golly I'm going to take it and sit here for an hour doing nothing."

While I love my work and find it a challenge, I also enjoy time off. I try to get my work done as efficiently as possible so I can get home earlier to spend time with my family. If I use my work time wisely, I still have time to coach my children's sports teams. I have time to get a workout, and I even find time for some true relaxation as opposed to taking time out in the middle of the workday to try to relax.

One of the easiest ways to take a giant step forward in any part of your life is to replace one bad habit with one good habit. Suppose you drink six colas or six cups of coffee a day. This is not a good habit. You are putting too much sugar and caffeine in your body, and that is not good for you. Instead of drinking six cups of coffee or colas, you could drink six glasses of water each day. That would make a huge impact in the way you feel. You would probably drop a few pounds and your overall health would improve.

You can apply the same principle at work. You can quit spending the first one sixteenth of the day getting ready for work. Instead, you turn on the light, skip the coffeepot and the chitchat and go straight to work. At the end of the day, work until quitting time. If you have organized your work throughout the day, it is not necessary to spend several minutes "getting ready" to leave. A simple "have a good evening" is enough closure with your coworkers, and you can say that on your way out the door, after you have turned off the light. Instead of "taking" a lunch hour, combine your lunchtime with something constructive. These new habits could increase your productivity by 25 percent. You will find that an added benefit from the change will be that time passes much faster. At the end of the day you feel good about how much you have accomplished, and you can leave work at the office and go home for a pleasant evening or weekend with family and friends. You will feel better about yourself, and the company will appreciate you more when you operate on the principle of "There is No Off Switch on a Tiger." You will find yourself more energized; you will get more work done than ever before; you will make more money; and most of all, you will be able to go home earlier and enjoy all the things you work so hard for.

"There is No Off Switch on a Tiger" is the motto for many areas of my life. I am a sports enthusiast, and I take the "tiger" approach when I walk on a tennis court or softball field. I am going to scrape, scratch, dive and slide to do everything I can to help my team win. This enthusiastic approach is contagious, whether it's with an athletic team or with co-workers. I find that enthusiasm and a strong work ethic are contagious. Team members and co-workers will respond to your approach by adopting the "no off switch" approach, and everyone will be more productive.

There is nothing wrong with saying you have two speeds (ON and OFF) in the workplace. When you come to work, you turn the light on and you work. When you leave the office, you turn the light off and you stop work. It is important to be able to turn it on and off when you want to. It is true that there are times when I enjoy working at home and may do a little extra paperwork or make some phone calls. The key is to know how to turn it on, how to turn it off and to always give your very best effort and go full throttle when it is time to work.

Champions have winning habits. They do the fundamentals. The same applies in business. Good business fundamentals applied consistently every day create a winning company. So go all out and remember "There is No Off Switch on a Tiger!"

10

Our Attitude is
the Difference

When I started the Hatcher Agency in 1990, I spent a lot of time searching for the perfect slogan to put on our business cards, letterhead and envelopes.

As an insurance sales rep, the thing I found most frustrating was that insurance companies were often indifferent to the problems of their customers. Sometimes people who really needed insurance simply could not afford it. Many customers got upset when they were notified of a rate increase. Others were irate when they learned that the insurance company would not pay a claim they thought was covered.

As a customer service representative and salesperson I sometimes got calls from customers who were rude and angry. It seemed to me that one of the major problems in our industry was the bad attitude between customer and company.

While it is true that the Customer Service Representative sometimes can't do much about rates or pay a claim that is not covered, I felt that a caring attitude would sometimes have left the customer feeling less abused.

I was determined that employees at our agency would be more sensitive to customers. They would have a different attitude from those that I had seen at other companies. I was convinced that the attitude a company has toward its customers and to the public, more than any other factor, determines its success.

Thus, I adopted the slogan: "Our Attitude Is the Difference."

At the Hatcher Agency, we take that slogan very seriously. It means that all employees must have a good attitude all the time. Attitude is a habit, and it can't be turned on and off. The good attitude must be extended not only to customers and prospective customers, but also to vendors. It must be demonstrated in relationships with co-workers, in the home, and even with people who are total strangers.

Why total strangers? First of all, because a good attitude makes life more pleasant for everybody. But there is another reason. It's good for business. If I eliminated all the "total strangers" I have gotten business from, our agency might be 33 percent smaller. I often meet people at a social gathering, on the street, or coaching a child in soccer and find out three or four years later that person has become the decision maker at an account I've been referred to. The way I treated that person when he was a stranger and the way I treat other people as strangers gets around and always comes back around. Having a good attitude toward all the people you come in contact with will not only make you feel better, it will also improve your business' bottom line.

Remember that the next time somebody cuts you off in traffic and you get ready to blow your horn and offer an obscene gesture.... That driver may be your largest customer or a future customer that you just lost.

Be forgiving in life and treat people with a good attitude whether they deserve it or not. You will feel better; you will not waste extra energy; and your business will be a lot more successful.

*I want a salesman that protects
my best interests, even if I don't know
what my best interests are. I want an
advisor that keeps me out of trouble.*

CHAPTER

"Outrageous Service" Means Saying No, Too

Have you heard that the latest advice on parenting is "Give your child whatever he or she wants?" Of course you haven't. That would be ridiculous.

It is just as ridiculous in the business world to believe that we should or can give our customers everything they request.

A good salesman and a good company must listen to what the client wants. But just as a good parent must use some judgment before honoring a child's request, a good company will sometimes protect the client from a bad business decision. The good sales person is in a position to know how to help the client save money or to choose the product that will work best for that company.

To illustrate my point: You go to a restaurant and order a hamburger, french fries and a drink. The cashier rings up the three items separately. Then you realize that the special that includes a sandwich, french fries and a drink costs much less. You got what you ordered, so you have no room for complaint. However, if the cashier had pointed out that the special was a better deal, you might have enjoyed your meal more; and you would certainly have felt better about returning to that restaurant. I have had experiences where the waiter suggested that it would be much more economical for me to order the package and that it even included dessert.

Why would the restaurant want to point out the better deal when it means they make less money and give away more food? The answer is simple. Sometimes not giving the customer what he orders can create a winning situation for everybody. In the case of the restaurant, the customer saves money and is happy with the service. He is likely to come back, so the owner gets more business. The waiter that pointed out the extra benefit will probably get an extra tip. Everybody wins.

A good company sells only good products, but not all products are right for every customer. Although the industry you are in may be nothing like the restaurant business, there will be times in your industry when you must educate your customers and point out the benefits of doing things differently from what they requested. There may be times when a customer will demand that you do something a certain way, and you are certain that this is a wrong decision, and that it will cause major problems down the road. At this point, you must be willing to simply stand strong and tell the customer that you would be doing him a disservice if you sold him the product. You can do this with confidence if the customer knows he can trust you to do what is right for him.

Being able to say no to the customer requires that the sales representative be educated about the products he or she sells. If you refuse to sell a "wrong" product, you must be able to suggest a "right" one. A good rule of thumb is to suggest the product you would use if you were in their position. If the customer insists on taking a shortcut and wants to buy a product that may cause grief later on, you may want to put in writing any problems you think could result from the purchase.

Consistent and genuine concern for the customer's interest builds a mutual trust that ensures repeat business. "Outrageous Service" means getting customers what they want, advising them on the best deals, and protecting them from things that are not best for them.

CHAPTER

If I Were a Car Salesman, I Would Sell Cadillacs

I only sell the products that have the standards of quality I would want for myself. As an insurance salesman, I learned that living by this rule helps me to feel good about what I sell and about myself.

From time to time we have motivational speakers at our staff meetings. We recently had David Fortenberry, who is a top bond salesman in Little Rock and an employee of Regions Bank. The thing I remember most from his talk was that he said he never sold anything he would not buy for his own account. This is a good rule of operation for any company.

There are three reasons why, if I were a car salesman, I would sell Cadillacs.

First of all, if I were selling Cadillacs, I could certainly believe in my product. Cadillac has been the premiere car in America for many years. Its reputation for quality is such that when we refer to "the Cadillac" of an industry, we mean the very best that industry has to offer.

As a Cadillac salesman I would never have to worry about my product performing well. When people buy the very best product, they never look back and say "Boy, I wish I had bought something better" or "I wish I had bought something cheaper." There is an old and true saying that the thrill of the low price is soon forgotten in the loss of good quality.

When you sell the very best products, you sell to a clientele that has more dollars to spend, and they will spend them quicker and easier because they understand that good quality is actually cheaper in the long run. Even when times are tough, the Mercedes and Cadillac dealerships, the very best restaurants and the companies that provide the very best services generally survive. Good products, good companies and good people can survive the difficult times because providing the best services keeps them in demand.

There are people whose business is selling crummy products to strangers. These people obviously expect to make one-time sales and hope they will never see the customers again. I personally enjoy selling good products to people who are looking for an ongoing relationship with their vendor. I find that the kind of customers who shop around and buy the lowest price each and every time generally do not place a high value on quality and service. They don't want long-term business relationships. They are here today and gone tomorrow. Customers who look for quality will appreciate "Outrageous Service" and are much more likely to be long term and profitable customers.

You can design your company's products to attract the type of customers that you want to sell and retain. You will find that your business will not only be more profitable, it will be a lot more pleasant as well. Based on the fact that you will spend the majority of your life working in your profession, you might as well sell a product that you believe in and enjoy. Sell the Cadillac of your industry and reap the profits and personal rewards of a job well done.

Of course, there are more good products out there than the Cadillac and Mercedes. In fact, I drive a Chevrolet Suburban and Silverado truck and enjoy these fine automobiles. The point is to find and sell a fine product you believe in.

13

"When someone says, 'Let me be honest with you,' I always wonder: does that mean they have been dishonest with me all the other times? I expect you to be honest with me, so there is no sense announcing it."

– Joe Hatcher (my father)

Honesty is the Best Policy

Of all the men I have ever known, my father is the most honest. Some people would say he is honest to a fault. I must also say that my father is one of the most trusted men I have ever known. It is interesting how honesty and trust are always intertwined.

Telling the truth is not always easy. Sometimes the truth hurts people's feelings; other times it makes them very angry. I have learned, however, that even when people get hurt or angry, they know they can still trust me. On the other hand, if I am less than truthful and they find out the truth—as they almost inevitably will—they may never trust me again.

Trust is the most essential ingredient in any relationship, including business. Most of us would not buy anything from a salesman we don't trust. The most important asset a top salesperson can have is the trust of his client. There is only one way to gain trust for a long period of time, and that is with integrity and honesty. Honesty always has been and always will be the best policy. When you are honest, you can sleep better; you can look people in the eye; and you can feel good about yourself. Dishonesty, even little white lies, leads to bigger lies and the erosion of trust. Once trust is destroyed, it is almost impossible to rebuild.

Any organization that wants to offer "Outrageous Service" will teach its employees the importance of complete honesty. That means leveling with the boss, other employees and customers even when they have blown it, no matter how bad the mistake. If one of my employees who made a mistake lies about what he has done, his job is definitely in jeopardy. However, the employee who levels with me, even if the mistake is a major one, will get another chance to prove that he can do the job.

Let's say an employee who is always honest with me makes a horrible mistake, and even repeats the mistake over and over again. Maybe the mistakes are costing the company so much money I can't afford to leave the employee in that job. However, because he is honest, I will try to find a job in another area that fits his abilities and needs.

Employees who are honest and trustworthy are valuable assets in any company. When you reward these qualities, employees generally respond with a deep sense of loyalty to you and to the company. In today's business world all employers can use more people who are honest, trustworthy and loyal.

Leveling with the customer is as important as being honest with the boss. I have had to call a customer and confess that I just flat forgot to do something I agreed to do. I have admitted that we blew it on a particular project and made a horrible mistake. I have acknowledged my embarrassment that we made this type of mistake. What does this kind of confession do to the relationship? Well, it is hard to argue with confession and repentance. When a person says, "Look, I just blew it; I made a mistake; I don't have any excuses; I'm sorry," there is not much room for argument. No one can say "You are a liar," or "That excuse is not good enough." Requesting forgiveness and being forgiving can be a humbling experience for both parties and can build empathy and trust between people who have similar goals.

What we do after we have made a major mistake and apologized for it is to correct the mistake and reimburse the client for any inconvenience we may have caused. The reimbursement may be in the form of cash, or it may be a better product or more service. The key is to fix the problem so that it is a little better than if we had not made the mistake to begin with. Almost without exception, leveling with the customer will mean we have a good chance of keeping that customer. If we do not tell the truth, we may have to cover our tracks for years. The customer who learns, even years later, that he has been deceived is almost certain to terminate the relationship.

To err is human. And your customers are human too. They make mistakes; they have employees that are not always honest and trustworthy; and yes, customers are sometimes less than honest. When customers make mistakes, you have an opportunity to be magnanimous and forgiving. If they, like you, want to move to the very top, they will learn that honesty is the best policy.

Honesty is not only the best policy; it is also less stressful in the long run. Perhaps that is the meaning of the Bible verse: "You shall know the truth and the truth shall set you free."

CHAPTER

14

Swim Upstream

Even a dead fish can swim downstream. The fish (and the people) that get noticed are the ones that swim upstream. The goal here is to stand out in a positive way rather than in a negative way. In the current business market, it is easy to stand out from the crowd that uses voice mail to answer telephones and provides impersonal and lackadaisical service, where trust and a promise are only as good as the legal contracts that the attorneys can defend.

Oh how I love this market! Because I am willing to swim upstream and offer Outrageous Service, I am able to go where very few people get to go. I am willing to do the extras and be super successful.

In order to see the difference swimming upstream can make, let's look at an industry that is well known for its poor service and communication. Anyone who has ever had a home remodeled knows how difficult it is to find a construction business that offers outstanding— or even acceptable—service.

Rarely does a construction person sit down with you and go over the bid, explaining to you how much each item will cost and how he arrived at the bottom line price. Generally, you get more than one bid; and you choose the low one, expecting to get quality service. The construction workers show up late for the job or do not show up at all. They make a mess that they leave for you to clean up after they leave. They put their greasy hands all over your light switches and doorknobs and even on your walls. They drag mud and dirt into your house and urinate on your toilet seat when they use the restroom. (Obviously not all of these things happen every time, and there are some construction companies that are committed to doing an outstanding job; however, they are in the minority.)

Imagine how much business you could get if you started a construction company that offered "Outrageous Service." You sit down with your customers to explain the cost, and you agree that the cost will not increase. You agree to eat the cost if you come out over budget and to refund the money if you come out under budget. Your crews show up on time like clockwork and make a habit of cleaning up every last speck of sawdust at the end of the day. They remember that the customer has to live in the house while it is under construction. They keep their hands and feet clean so they don't damage the customer's house. They basically spend the majority of their time trying to make things convenient for the customer in addition to doing a good job. They communicate with the customer about the progress of the project and the expected completion date. They let the customer know that they empathize with them and that they are making every effort to finish things on time. Any construction company that did all of these things would stand out and would certainly be like a fish swimming upstream. They would be going one way while the majority of construction companies are going the other.

All the rules that apply to the construction company will work for any industry. A great way to improve your success quickly is to sit down and make a list of the services your particular company provides and see how they compare to your competition. You will probably find that you and the rest of the industry competition are offering the same products with approximately the same level of service. That means the only thing you have to separate yourself from the competition is cost.

One way to eliminate your competition quickly is to start taking a look at your basic services and see how you can swim upstream to deliver the kind of service no one else offers. You may have to increase your prices a little to cover the extra cost, but most people are willing to pay more when they know they are getting good service. When you swim upstream and offer "Outrageous Service," you build the kind of reputation that does not require bidding against the competition. People will seek you out because a colleague or a neighbor has told them about you. When people are seeking quality service, a strong referral from a satisfied customer is more important than the lowest price.

When I hire someone to do a construction project, it is important that they can get the job done right. But it is just as important that they are reliable and dependable and that they communicate with me. I have worked with talented builders who did not come to work on time and who did not communicate with me during the project. Given a choice, I would hire a less talented builder who communicated with me and was there on time. A builder who listens to me, who shows up on time, and who communicates with me as the job progresses proves that he is trying to do what is in my best interest. Even if he makes mistakes initially, I know I can count on him to eventually fix them. When your company is willing to swim upstream and provide extra services, people will view you as the only choice, and you will spend less time submitting bids and more time doing work.

At The Hatcher Agency we swim upstream in several ways compared to other insurance companies. We swim upstream by answering the phone with a live person. Our customers don't get connected with voice mail unless they request it. We deliver our clients donuts in the morning and cookies in the afternoon; we make goodwill calls every month just to see how our clients are doing. We have a full-time courier to get information and products to our clients quickly. We find ways to get claims paid for clients instead of trying to find ways to get around paying claims. We look for ways to do all the paperwork for our clients instead of leaving it for them to do. All of these services don't cause us to increase our price, because the prices are already set by the insurance companies. Because the price is the same with us as with another agent, the customer will buy from us if we deliver better service. In other words, service is the differential.

In your business you can find many ways to swim upstream. When you make the changes to swim upstream, you will stand out; and you may be swimming alone. But, it will be a very successful and enjoyable swim.

Note: I have worked with many outstanding construction people in remodeling my homes over the years (Jack Hartsell, H&O Remodeling) and know many corporate contractors that do a great job, but at the same time most of us have also worked with the home remodelers who simply don't show up for work at all.

PART TWO

"Outrageous Service" Tools

CHAPTER

15

A Two-Dollar Bill for a One Percent Improvement

I am a big fan of Tom Peters and all the books he has written on management and business success. One thing I remember reading was that Tom Peters said you only have to be one percent better than your competition on a regular basis to get all the business. If you play 30 basketball games in a season and in each game you score 100 points and your opponent scores 99 points, you will be 30 – 0 and become the national champion. Fine tuning a few extra details can make you better than your competition. In business if you are one percent better, you can get all the business since customers generally do not split their business between two vendors for one product.

At The Hatcher Agency we have staff meetings every Tuesday morning at 7:00 a.m. During that staff meeting I ask each of our employees to bring a one percent improvement suggestion on how we can better serve the customer. Each week I get several good suggestions, and I reward people for good ideas that they have implemented during the week. The reward is nothing big, but for each new idea or "Outrageous Service" they deliver during the week I give them a $2 bill and reward them in front of their peers. These $2 bills given out during the course of the year provide a little extra pocket change for our employees and produce huge results for our company. The practice keeps everybody searching for better ways to serve the customer. I do not give out $2 for every suggestion or for every service that an employee gives to a customer during the week. I am the sole judge and jury, and I decide when I think a service is beyond ordinary and when a new idea is worth implementing. But the $2 incentive and the recognition that the employees get keeps everyone working to improve our company.

If the reward were $100, I think it would provide the wrong incentives and cause too much competition among employees. The $2 bill seems to work out just right for us. In order to build the best service it can, a company must constantly look and listen and encourage employees to bring forth new ideas that will make a difference. It is not enough to ask them to do this at an annual retreat; the practice must have an ongoing format that is measured and followed up.

Here is a story that shows how "Outrageous Service" can help your bottom line. A national pizza franchise became amazed after noticing that one of the franchise stores continually outperformed their other stores month after month, year after year. They decided to go to this small town and find out what the pizza franchise was doing so much better than the others were doing. What they found was that each week the manager of the pizza franchise had a staff meeting with his delivery people. In the pizza business the delivery people are the ones who see the customer; and therefore, they are the salesmen or the most important players on the pizza team. Each week this sales manager asked the delivery people who did the most outrageous wonderful thing for the customer that week, and he would reward them with $20 bills, $50 bills and $100 bills—depending on the week.

The delivery people would come back with stories like "I delivered the pizza with paper plates and napkins, and I served the first slice of pizza to them." Another person might say, "They ordered a Coke so I brought them a glass with ice in it." Someone else said he delivered the pizza and left the customers some coupons so they could get a discount on their next pizza.

The franchise noticed that as these delivery people competed to see who could deliver the most "Outrageous Service" people were not ordering pizza from the franchise anymore; they were ordering it from Jimmy, John or Barry. The families liked the delivery person so much they wanted him to deliver their pizza each week.

This pizza franchise had found a way to give its pizza a personality as well as good taste. Of course, the pizza delivery people got much larger tips, which made them even more enthusiastic about doing a great job for the franchise. All of this resulted from an owner deciding to give incentives to encourage his employees to come up with better ways of delivering the product. The answers are out there for your company too if you will set up a regular format to get them.

CHAPTER

16

Five "Thank You" Notes per Week

How many "thank you" notes did you receive last year? I am not talking about "thank you"s for gifts you gave someone, but notes just for something nice you did or for the good work you did for someone. You may not be able to count five for the entire year. Too few people take the time to say "thank you" to others for acts of kindness or for work well done.

At The Hatcher Agency every employee is required to write five "thank you" notes a week. This is to let the people we deal with each day know that we appreciate them. Taking time to thank vendors, customers, friends and neighbors for the little things they do to help us achieve our goals accomplishes three things:

1. The person receiving the note feels very good about it.
2. We feel good for having written the note.
3. The person who receives the note becomes a friend and ally who will help us even more in the future.

Writing "thank you" notes is a win/win situation for everyone involved, and in today's tough competitive business climate we can't afford to pass up an opportunity for a win/win situation. If all 23 people in the agency write at least 5 thank you notes per week, the agency is sending out over 5,900 notes per year. That is 5,900 better relationships cultivated every single year.

I have found that to be successful with anything for a long period of time we must monitor the results and keep score. For this reason, we require each employee to turn in a list of the people they write each week and note the relationship we have with those people. Occasionally, employees write "thank you" notes to family members and friends. These notes improve family relationships, which makes the employee happier and more productive. For the most part, however, our employees write "thank you" notes to their vendors and customers.

Vendors are often an overlooked part of the successful business formula. Good vendor service is essential to good customer service. We really try to focus on the fact that we need to treat our vendors just as if they were our clients. Taking time to say "thank you" to vendors can have tremendous results.

One of the things I like most to hear is that a vendor has called or written and requested to buy insurance from us. This happens frequently because we treat our vendors so well that they cannot imagine how well we would treat them as customers. I understand this reaction because I like to do business with customers who treat me well.

Specifically, I have had two auto dealerships who treated me so well as their insurance agent that when it came time to buy a car, I bought it from them. They have earned the sale regardless of the price. Because they have always treated me right, I know they will take care of me on the price too. When a customer wants to buy from you, you can almost always make the sale.

One of the first things to remember when delivering "Outrageous Service" is that everyone in the world is a potential customer and a potential referral source. Saying "thank you" to everyone involved in your business and providing outstanding service to everyone you meet results in the kind of good will that benefits everybody.

Write a minimum of five "thank you" notes a week and let people know how much you appreciate them. I average writing 20 "thank you" notes a week because I am truly grateful to all the people who help me every day.

Donuts in the Morning;
Cookies in the Afternoon

What do donuts and cookies have to do with the insurance business? Nothing, really. That's why they work as well for any business as they do for us.

When we meet with a client, we want it to be a friendly meeting that our clients look forward to. Almost all meetings with clients are pretty similar. They start with a handshake; everybody is dressed up in business attire; there are a few comments about the weather or how cute the kids' pictures are, and compliments on the new tie you are wearing. To a sophisticated sales person and customer these typical comments are pretty dull and monotonous. At the Hatcher Agency, we add a little "taste" to the meeting. When we see a customer in the morning, we bring a box of donuts with our Hatcher Agency label affixed to it. If we meet in the afternoon, each person present gets a bag of our Hatcher Agency Chocolate Chip or Macadamia Nut Cookies.

Our sales people don't walk in and start the conversation by commenting on ties or photographs. If they truly like the tie or the picture of the kids, they can mention that later. But, as icebreakers, those comments are so stale that no one takes them seriously. We have found that cookies and donuts make our meeting a little less formal and more comfortable for both ourselves and for the customer. Since we spend a lot of our time in meetings, we might as well make them fun.

It is hard to schedule lunches with all your clients on a regular basis, but donuts and cookies make every meeting with a client an opportunity to show them you appreciate them. Over all the years of having different meetings with clients, I would say that in 80 percent of the cases, the client eats the donuts or cookies during the presentation. We never give our donuts and cookies to a client and say, "We brought donuts because we really appreciate you." That is too much and too phony. The small gift is not big enough to make them feel obligated to purchase from us, but it is enough to show that we appreciate the opportunity to meet with them.

We are convinced that serving donuts or cookies gets meetings off to a better start. Customers and prospective customers who have been "treated" are more open and give us the information we need more quickly. They are more likely to give us information that helps us make the sale. The Hatcher Agency donuts and cookies have become a trademark of our company that everybody recognizes. Customers know when they see us there will be donuts in the morning and cookies in the afternoon. Many clients who are scheduled to meet with us in the morning don't eat breakfast because they know they will be served at the meeting. Clients who have a meeting with us following lunch sometimes do not order dessert because they know the cookies are on the way.

We take our cookies to an even higher level. When our delivery person delivers any item to anyone, he includes a bag of chocolate chip or macadamia nut cookies. New customers who call our agency and order claim forms may expect to receive them in the mail a couple of days later. Imagine their surprise when a courier shows up with the forms in an envelope with a bag of chocolate chip cookies? Most of our customers are quite impressed and really appreciate the personal service. If our courier delivered a speeding or parking ticket to the police station, it would go with a bag of cookies. (Unfortunately for me, we've fed the police department too many times.) There is absolutely no one that comes in contact with our courier that does not get a bag of cookies. If a person is in a car wreck in front of our office and has to come in to use the phone, we give him a bag of cookies. The Hatcher Agency cookies have become well known and we have had many companies call us and copy our cookie delivery idea. It is a great little gift to let people know that you are a little different and that you care about them.

Many times in my career I have been introduced to a particular person for the first time at a party and that person said "Yes, I know you. You are the man with the cookies. Your courier gave me a bag of cookies one day when I ran into him." These cookies have put many smiles on our customers' faces because they are an unexpected gift of appreciation delivered not by the president, but in most people's eyes by one of the lowest level employees in our company, our courier. Other companies give away pens and post-it notes, etc., but I have found nothing better to give away than cookies and donuts. Food is universally appreciated.

As I wrote the last sentence I realized that there are some exceptions. We have a couple of customers who are diabetics and when we have appointments with those customers, we take bananas and animal crackers instead of donuts or cookies. Those customers are appreciative and know we are paying attention and delivering truly "Outrageous Service" by thinking of their special condition. You should see the smiles on their faces when we show up with that banana or animal crackers. When you show customers that you are conscious of these kinds of details, they know they can count on you for the big decisions about their insurance or whatever product you are selling.

Starting a meeting with a snack won't guarantee a contract or agreement, but it is certainly a good way to get started.

CHAPTER

Holiday Cards

Sure enough, it is Holiday time again! Do a little survey this year and keep all the holiday cards you receive. More than likely, 95 percent of the holiday cards you receive from businesses will be pre-printed business cards with either the company's name or a generic message typed inside and possibly a signature, at best. When I receive a holiday card like this, it tells me that I am on that particular company's vendor list, that someone has signed a thousand holiday cards hurriedly and a secretary has stuffed them in an envelope. They paid $1.00 or more for the holiday card and paid the postage to get it to me. While I appreciate being on their list, I do not feel that I have been delivered the personal touch or "Outrageous Service" at holiday time.

When I started The Hatcher Agency, I wrote a personal note in every single holiday card that went out. As our agency grew, the number of cards I sent increased. After writing 1,000 personal notes on holiday cards one year, I realized that the day was coming when I could no longer physically do this. However, I did not want to send out holiday cards that were not personal; and I wanted the holiday cards that we spend a great deal of money and effort on to have an impact. Then one year an insurance company sent me a postcard with a picture of all the employees who serviced our account. Out of the approximately 500 holiday cards I received from companies that year, theirs was the only one with a photo on it. It was my favorite because it gave me a chance to see all the people we worked with, many of whom were in the home office and I had never met. The card seemed very personal to me, and it made me eager to talk to the company again so I could tell them that I now knew what they looked like.

At holiday time we all get cards from our friends with pictures of their kids or families on them. When we receive these cards from our friends, they seem very personal and the pictures are generally circulated among the closest of friends. Each year it is good to see how the kids of all our friends throughout the country are growing up. Most families sign the card or even have the picture card printed up with a slogan like, "Merry Christmas from the Jones." As long as there is a picture involved, it seems like a personal card and we enjoy getting it and studying it. Our agency decided to try the same approach with our holiday card. The results were outstanding.

Virtually every customer we saw after the holiday season thanked us for the card and commented on how nice it was to see everybody in the picture. We had a professional photographer take the photo, and the card was done first-class with a special message inside and all the employees' signatures. On the back of the photo, of course, each employee was identified so customers could look up the particular employee they worked with at our agency. The picture holiday card is personal and makes a normally mundane business card stand out.

Most of these holiday cards are hand delivered along with T-shirts (see chapter 20) to our clients each year. Printing the photo holiday card allows us, as we get larger, to stay personal when it is no longer possible for me to write a personal message to every customer and vendor during the holiday season. Our holiday picture varies each year. It may be formal or very informal; it may be a pose with Santa Claus or around the fireplace at my home. The variety gives our customers different views of us, and our customers enjoy the added personal touch. Following are our cards from the past two years.

THE HATCHER AGENCY
"Our Attitude is the Difference"

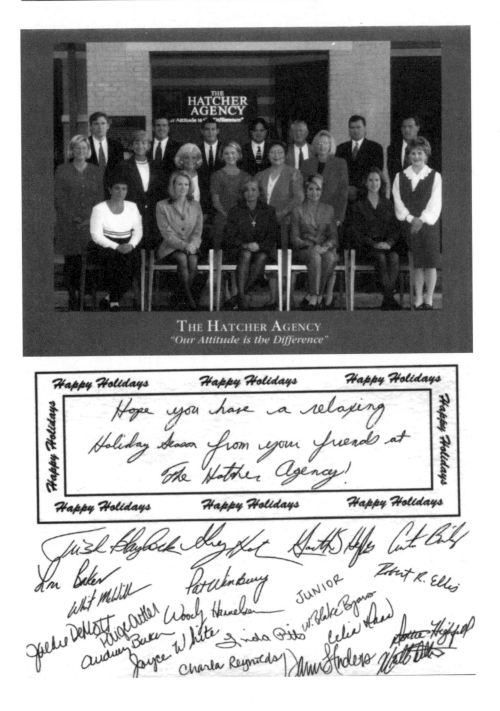

THE HATCHER AGENCY
"Our Attitude is the Difference"

CHAPTER

Progress Notes

The Progress Notes page is the first sheet of paper in all our client files. They are very similar to a doctor's records on a patient. The Progress Notes detail significant visits with the client and remind us of important conversations and events of each visit. They also detail each year's renewal, including any rate increase or decrease and the group's reaction to the change. We may list that in 1996 this client received a 6 percent rate increase on their health insurance; that in 1997 they received no rate increase; and in 1998 they received a 20 percent rate increase. The key is that the Progress Notes page is a running summary of all the things that have occurred with the client.

Every company needs to have progress notes on each client for the same reason a doctor needs medical records. Writing down information about previous visits and problems helps us get to know our clients better. The Progress Notes page provides a quick update for the salesman and service representative just before they see the client. One of the quickest and surest ways to lose a customer's confidence is going to a meeting and forgetting something important that you promised. Or, worse, having them remind you of something you discussed at the last meeting. When you forget details, the client is likely to doubt your ability to be thorough with the account. Why would they believe they are a top priority account when you cannot remember the information that is important to them?

Simply put, Progress Notes are just another way of writing down the important things that we need to know about our clients. Our files have two-hole metal clasps that hold these important papers in order. When you open a Hatcher Agency file, you can count on the progress notes page being first, and then we actually have a system of preference order for other memos and letters. This arrangement makes it easy for anyone servicing an account to find information quickly. Accounts can be easily transferred from one service representative to another because the new person will immediately have all the client information from day one to the present date. If you don't have a Progress Note system for your accounts, I advise you to set up one now. It can be an invaluable tool for servicing accounts and for passing on information in a systematic manner.

Progress Notes	
Date	Notes
7/6/98	Met with Jim & Susie to go over their renewal. They decided to stay with Blue Cross on their current plan after a 3% increase. (GH)
8/5/98	Did a group enrollment meeting to re-explain benefits and allow new employees to enroll for the group's 9/1 anniversary date. (GH)
8/27/98	Delivered new health ID cards to Susie and helped solve a claim problem for Jim Winter. (JD)

20

Everybody Loves a T-shirt

Cookies and donuts are great for meetings and daily deliveries, but what do you do for Christmas? We go right to the heart with an item that virtually everybody loves. The T-shirt, of course! I do not know many Americans that do not enjoy relaxing and lounging around in a 100 percent cotton T-shirt. So, for the past several years, our clients have received T-shirts from us at Christmas.

The T-shirts are always first quality made of 100% cotton, generally a Hanes Beefy T. Our logo, The Hatcher Agency, with our slogan, "Our Attitude Is The Difference" is on the front. On the back is a message that is strong and clear to anyone who ever sees the T-shirt. We rotate the slogans from year to year, but last year we put, "You can have everything in life you want if you will help enough other people get what they want." – By Zig Ziglar.

The T-shirts accomplish several things for our customers and our company. These include:

1. The customers become aware that they received gifts from few other vendors this year.
2. The gift is big enough to let them know we care about them, but is not large enough to make them feel obligated to buy from us.
3. Since the T-shirts are top quality, we send out the message that we are a top-notch company.
4. The slogan on the back of the T-shirt sends a message about our attitude that shows we are a very customer-oriented agency.

We are constantly amazed at the places our Hatcher Agency T-shirts go. I see them often at athletic clubs and other places.

Recently the building of one of our clients burned. When the television station interviewed the owner following the fire, there he was in his Hatcher Agency T-shirt. He was lounging around at home wearing the shirt when he was notified of the fire. The day the piece was aired on TV I got calls from many friends and clients letting me know that they had just seen one of our T-shirts on TV at the site of an insurance loss.

Not long ago one of our insurance carriers called me one hour before the start of the Boston Marathon. He left a message that he was going to wear our black long-sleeved Hatcher Agency T-shirt the first 11 miles of the race. For the last 15 miles he would change to the short-sleeved white model with the slogan, "There is no off-switch on a Tiger," on the back. For the record, Brian Dillion with Unum Life finished the marathon in just over 4 hours. Just imagine how many people saw those advertisements!

In the past we have given other gifts at Christmas, but they are always unique. One year, we gave pottery that my brother, an artist, made. Some companies spend a lot of money on cheese trays and fruit baskets, and soon after the holiday the customer can't remember who sent what. Our gifts last a long time and are reminders that we are a caring company.

One of the things that makes our Christmas T-shirts special is that we never mail them to in-state clients. Each shirt is personally delivered with our Christmas card. The service representative who handles the account delivers the gift with a personal wish for a Merry Christmas.

We give out over one thousand T-shirts every year and we get a lot of requests from people who have seen someone wearing one. There is no question that the T-shirt has been our most popular Christmas gift.

When other people see the T-shirt, they realize the uniqueness of The Hatcher Agency. I can't think of a better way to advertise.

Voice Mail
by Request Only

Today's world of computers and electronic media affords every company an incredible opportunity to provide extraordinary customer service. Unfortunately, that same technology has the potential for providing your customers with worse, less personal service.

Voice mail is an example of technology that can totally depersonalize the contact between a company and its customers.

This is an example of a scenario I have experienced many times. I call a company and get a secretary who is in a hurry to get off the line. (Maybe she is very busy; maybe she has too many lines to answer; maybe she just doesn't like to answer phones.) "Sure," she says, "John is in his office, let me connect you." The next thing you hear is John's 45 second recording on his voice mail box. More often than not, the voice mail is out of date. John may say he will be out of the office until the 16th, and you are calling on the 18th. Is he in or not?

When this happens to me, I find myself smashing down the operator button on my phone to get back to the secretary and ask if John Smith is physically in the office and if she could page him or find him. Needless to say, neither John nor his company has made a good impression.

When you call The Hatcher Agency, you get a human being. If the employee is out, you will have the option of leaving a message with the secretary or being connected with voice mail. If the employee is in, the secretary will find him. If he is on another line, you will be given the option of holding until he is available, leaving a message, or being connected to voice mail. If your call is urgent, the secretary may leave her chair and put a message under the employee's nose to let him or her know you are holding.

The only way you get voice mail at The Hatcher Agency is to request it. It is very important that voice mail be offered only as an option that you choose rather than as a way for the receptionist to get you off the line.

In many businesses today callers are basically told or encouraged to leave messages on voice mail. When I call and the person I want to speak with is busy or on another line, I will tell the secretary if I wish to be connected to voice mail. I want the option of leaving a message with a person.

Many companies are continually looking for ways to make things convenient for themselves instead of for their customers. A company that wants to give people service the old-fashioned way will look at what is most convenient for the customer, starting with the phone lines. This is one of those "little things" we can do to make a huge impression on current customers and prospects.

I can think of no industry worse about voice mail than the insurance industry. When I call the insurance companies I work with, 90 percent of the time I reach a voice mail recording either on the initial reception or when trying to be connected to a specific person. I have to punch through all the different buttons and go through all the mazes to finally run the person down. When customers of The Hatcher Agency have an insurance problem, they can call our agency and always get through to a person the first time. That is a huge selling point.

To make sure that our callers never receive a busy signal, we always have more phones lines than we have people working. Even though it costs a little extra to make sure nobody ever receives unsatisfactory service from the very first ring, it's worth it. Voice mail should be an option by request only, never a method used to replace the personal service that only people can provide.

CHAPTER

22

We Deliver

Can you imagine an insurance agency having a full-time courier? At The Hatcher Agency we consider it one of our most important services and one that can be implemented in any industry.

How much time do we spend each day getting the car filled with gas; picking up a prescription medicine or dry cleaning; delivering a last second letter, proposal, or memorandum; picking up the mail; making the daily deposit; getting the mail out at the end of each day, picking up that special gift for a client's family member, getting the last second birthday card—or any one of a hundred errands that can distract us from having a productive work day? Multiply that by 23 employees, and you can certainly see the need for a business to have a delivery person or courier.

Part of our overall attitude in regard to service at The Hatcher Agency is that all employees have to run errands, some of a personal nature, that must be done during the work day because that is the only time the other businesses are open.

If I have a group of employees making $30,000 to $50,000-plus running errands when we can have someone in the $20,000 range running these errands, then I can actually save money for the company. We can also deliver more "Outrageous Service" that is way beyond the expectations of our customers. Our courier is equipped with a pager and a car phone, so we can call him on the road at any time. We save a lot of time by calling him when something comes up that he can add to his list. Having the courier make an extra stop has saved many hours for our employees—hours that can be used to make us a more productive agency.

I must admit that the fact we have a courier is not something I really planned. Actually, it is something that I stumbled into. Just eight years ago our courier was a person who lived on the streets.

Junior, as we call him, had no home. He spent some nights at the Salvation Army's shelter, but most nights he slept on the back porch of the office building we moved into when we started the company. Junior was different from most street persons in that he was extremely friendly; but he had been out of work for over seven years, and for the last four years had lived on the streets. I got to know him when he startled me by wishing me good morning as I arrived at the office one day at 6:00 a.m. A couple of months after this initial meeting and the greetings I received every morning, I took him home with me. My wife gave him a haircut; he took his first shower in over four years, and he had Thanksgiving dinner with us.

This small gesture on my part during a holiday weekend has turned out to be one of the best business moves I ever made. Following the dinner, I worked out a deal with one of my clients who had a janitorial service to hire Junior who worked for him for the next two years doing janitorial work for a local radio station. For these two years I received his paychecks and paid his bills, got him an apartment and basically took care of his day-to-day needs. Junior could not read or write and certainly was not very good with financial matters. In addition to paying his bills, I gave him spending money each week so I could keep him on a tight budget and keep him off the streets.

When my friend decided to get out of the janitorial business, Junior was left without a job. Despite the good progress that Junior made as a janitor, there was no way that I could ever see employing him with my company. He was still not clean or professional looking enough to work with our clients. We searched and searched for another job for him, but no other company wanted to take the risk of hiring him either. Finally, I decided that Junior could drive me to all my appointments while I sat in the back seat and did my paperwork. This saved me countless hours; and after all, I was still paying his bills even though he had no income. I thought I might as well get something for my money.

We got Junior some new clothes and required that he be showered and smelling good each and every day. Some days he did not do this and we sent him home; but eventually he improved to the point where we could count on him to show up in a professional manner each day. I started having him run errands for me when he was not driving me to appointments; and before we realized it, our full-time courier was born.

Now that our agency has 23 employees, Junior never has a down moment. There is always something for him to do, a package to deliver, a car to get the oil changed on, clothes to pick up at the cleaners, and paperwork to be delivered to our clients and carriers. Junior has now worked for our company for six years and is one of our most valuable employees. I can't think of anyone in the Agency who would be harder to replace because Junior is totally committed to doing the job, and we don't have to worry about constant turnover.

We recently moved Junior into his own three-bedroom home, and he drives a brand new Hatcher Agency pickup truck with a car phone and pager. Junior has come a long way, but he has also helped The Hatcher Agency come a long way in delivering truly "Outrageous Service." As you can see from the picture at the beginning of the chapter, "Our Attitude is the Difference" is printed on the side of the truck. The back of the truck reads "Home of Outrageous Service." And this is what Junior delivers to our clients every day.

The Enrollment Van

The best way to start this chapter is to show you a picture of our enrollment van. As you can see, it has our Hatcher Agency logo on the front and side. On the back it reads again, "The Home of Outrageous Service."

Every company that has employees pays mileage allowances when employees use their own vehicle to go out and meet the customer. I discovered that paying money for mileage expenses was hard to control. Additionally, employees were often driving to see clients in cars that were not equipped with a car phone, or their car was not clean enough to project the image I wanted to our clients. I calculated that for the money I was paying each month in mileage reimbursements, I could make a payment on a van. Now all our employees can drive a nice vehicle that is always clean, completely serviced and full of gas. The van is stocked with all the enrollment materials our employees need so they don't have to repack for each trip. It also has a stock of our famous Hatcher Agency cookies, so employees always have the cookies available when they call on clients. The van delivers a strong message of service to our clients.

I find that our employees prefer a company car. They really did not like driving their own cars when we went on multi-state enrollments. Even though they got reimbursed, they didn't like putting the wear and tear on their personal cars.

The Hatcher Agency enrollment van has traveled throughout the South delivering "Outrageous Service" as we do multi-site enrollment meetings for our groups. It is equipped with a car phone for safety and convenience. It is also stocked with maps for guidance to the client site and all the supplies necessary for enrollment. When we need to entertain a client, the van is clean, and accommodates more people than the typical car.

Many clients have commented on seeing our enrollment van traveling the streets. It serves as a good advertisement of the service we are delivering to our clients.

The only two drawbacks that I considered when I purchased the van were:

1. What if somebody has a wreck driving the company van?
2. What if someone drives the van in an impolite manner? We are sticking our necks out when we print "The Home of Outrageous Service" on the back of a van. If we fail to deliver the outrageous service we advertise, we could cause ourselves a lot of grief.

I checked with my property and casualty agent, and he informed me that the company's liability is the same whether the employee is driving a personal car or a company car. We already had insurance that covered the damage for anyone driving on company business regardless of who owned the vehicle.

Instead of worrying about the second issue, I decided I would be sure employees get the message about the importance of being considerate on the highway. While "The Home of Outrageous Service" is a bold claim to print on our delivery vehicle, it is not an idea that is new to our employees. They know that we have to deliver what we promise, and they have never let me down. In fact, they are quite proud of the van. Our staff, like all good work forces, wants to do a good job; and take pride in their work. The Hatcher Agency enrollment van is just another tool we use to deliver "Outrageous Service."

The toughest thing about
being a success is that you have
to keep being a success.

CHAPTER

Goodwill Calls

The Goodwill Call is a Hatcher Agency trademark and one that separates us from virtually any business I have ever known. Many times when I present a proposal to a customer I ask them to name one vendor they have bought a product from that called them every single month afterward just to see how they were doing. I have yet to be told by any customer that they have ever had a vendor treat them in this positive way. Sometimes an appliance company will call you every month after the purchase to see if you want to buy the extended warranty. While this is certainly follow up, it is not the type of follow up we do on our Goodwill Calls.

Each service representative in our company is required to call each of their clients each month just to see how the client is doing. Even if the client has called us 25 times that month on other service issues, they still receive one call from our staff each month to check in on them. The representative may have new information on their particular insurance carrier or on something that is going on in the market that the client may be interested in. If a client has more than 25 employees, we visit them in person once a month. These Goodwill Calls help prevent major problems by identifying small problems before they become big ones, and they let the customer know we care about them. All of us as buyers appreciate a good salesman that follows up to check and see if the product we have purchased is satisfactory. Giving our customers an opportunity to talk to us at least once a month, even if they never have a service issue, helps keep us on their mind. Listening to customers is a service that is so beyond the norm that the customer will end up telling other people about this "Outrageous Service."

Each Goodwill Call is recorded on the computer and the service representative or salesman writes a short paragraph on what was discussed with the client. This report is printed out each month and I, the owner of the business, read every single Goodwill Call Report in every area of our company each month. The monthly Goodwill Call Report generally totals around 80 to 100 pages. It is worth my taking the time to read these reports, however, because I may find trends that are going on with our clients that we need to address. The Goodwill Call is our most important service tool because it keeps us in touch with our clients, helps prevent problems and gives the client the kind of service that is so unexpected it causes them to refer more business to us.

A page of a Goodwill Call Report is included here, with the names changed to protect our clients' confidentiality.

Goodwill Calls: June

Group Name	Executive Contact	Date Visited/ Phoned	Administrator	Phone Number	Notes
ABC Company	Charlie Chaplin (Monthly)	6/12	Marilyn Monroe	555-1246	Went to see Charlie at least 3 times this month: 1) to talk to his Hughes employees about health insurance 2) to pick up STD check from Marilyn 3) to pick up his sons bills/claims to work on. Everything is going well.
Roy's Restaurant	Roy Rogers	6/15	Dale Evans (Mar, Jun, Sep, Dec)	555-1000	Have been to Roy's a couple of times: 1) to deliver the employee packets 2) to pick up employee packets and deliver to QualChoice.
	Stan Laurel (Feb, May, Aug, Nov)				Stan is concerned because his son's doctor is not on the new list. I have QualChoice checking into it.
Anesthesia Clinic		6/15	Buffalo Bill	555-7812	Went to Conway to see Bill. Gave him the STD flier. Talked to him about the importance of LTD/STD. He was very nice and thought it was nice of me to drop by.
Acme Flying School	Wyle E. Coyote (Jan, Apr, Jul, Oct)		Fogg Horn	555-4888	Stopped by to visit. Wyle had an accident claim (broken leg) and was sent an accident form by Blue Cross. I instructed him to complete it quickly and return it to them for prompt claim processing.
Cardiology Clinic	Kathryn Hepburn (Monthly)	6/30	Louis Armstrong	555-7890	Visited with Kathryn and reminded her that her renewal is coming up and we are shopping with reinsurance carriers and fully insured carriers. She said the plan was working well.
XYZ Architects, Inc.	Frank Lloyd Wright (Jan, Apr, Jul, Oct)	6/25	Amelia Earhart	555-1586	Dropped by but Amelia was out for the week on vacation. Her son is looking at schools out of state and they were prospecting. We had an extra box of donuts so I brought it to them.
	Robert Mitchum (Feb, May, Aug, Nov)				

There is no greater loan
than a sympathetic ear.

Expressions of Sympathy

Nothing weighs on people quite like losing a loved one or having a special person critically ill. When you are in business you will often have clients, employees, vendors and associates who are experiencing serious crises. At The Hatcher Agency we try to keep up with our clients. If someone is sick or hurt or a death occurs in the family, the first person that hears about it starts a sympathy card. We all sign it and write a personal note in it. This small gesture lets the person know that we care. It also makes our entire staff feel good and helps us be aware of situations that are going on with people we care about. Sometimes we send plants or other gifts in addition to the card. At other times we have volunteered time or donated money. We try to do whatever it takes to let the people who support us know that we are there to help in difficult times.

Customers, vendors, friends—and yes, even our own employees— remember the way our agency treated them when they faced adversity.

Sympathy cards and gifts help remind us that it is not just business we are doing. None of us is going to be around forever, and it is the personal relationships that we develop that make us feel most fulfilled in our lives. Take time out to help people when they are down. Your efforts will be appreciated; but more importantly, everyone in your organization will feel good about it.

*If you don't get to know
your clients well, surely they can
find someone else who will.*

CHAPTER

The Blue Sheet

At The Hatcher Agency we have a service tool called the Blue Sheet. The Blue Sheet lists everything we would ever need to know about a particular client. This includes the client's name, phone number, fax number, e-mail address, street address, post office box and the names of our key contacts at the group. We enter this information into our computer system so all these people are easily accessible when we send out Christmas gifts, Christmas cards or general notices about changes in the agency. We also enter the birth date and Social Security number of each key contact. These are easy for us to obtain since they are on all insurance application forms. (In your business you may have to ask for the birth dates.) These dates are important to us because we send out birthday cards.

The other information your business would include on the Blue Sheet would depend on the kind of business you are in. Our Blue Sheet has all the information on the different insurance carriers the customer has and details the deductibles and benefits. If you are in the trucking business, for example, the Blue Sheet might detail what kind of cargo you ship for this client, what your prices are, and who their particular service representatives are. The important thing is that the Blue Sheet has all the details about your client. In essence, it's a cheat sheet on one two-sided page that gives you everything you need to know about the client. If you cannot get it all on one sheet front and back, then you use two sheets; but most companies will probably be able to cover the most critical information on each account using one page front and back. The page is printed on blue paper so it can be found in the file instantly.

Our Blue Sheet also lists directions on how to get to each account. This may seem trivial, but it can be a big deal when you consider the fact that a customer service representative may have 150 clients. If that representative leaves the company and a new one comes in, those directions can be extremely helpful. Calling the client to get directions may leave the impression the company is not very well organized.

We make extra photocopies of our Blue Sheets. One goes in the file and one goes to each service representative that handles the account. These Blue Sheets are even more effective than a computer. We have them in alphabetical order so when someone calls, the representative that handles 150 clients can flip to the Blue Sheet quickly and know immediately what the contact person's name is, and what their benefits are. Some companies feel it is a necessity to have this information on the computer, but I feel the Blue Sheet is more valuable. Although all the information on the Blue Sheet is on the computer and could be called up on several screens, it is not mobile like the Blue Sheet. If we go see a client, the Blue Sheet is in the file and we can pull it and have all the information we need right in front of us on one sheet of paper.

The Blue Sheet could also list critical information such as the names of your client's children or spouse and other important information that everybody needs to know. The Blue Sheet is an invaluable asset to every corporation. If you have a customer worth keeping, it is worth your time to keep this critical information. Develop your own Blue Sheet that fits your company, give it out to your service representatives and watch the efficiency of your company grow.

NOTE: I have included a copy of our Blue Sheet to help you in developing your own tool.

GROUP SUMMARY SHEET FOR ABC COMPANY

Service Representative:		Rater:	

GROUP INFORMATION

Completed by:	Date:	Entered By:	Date:

Name ID :	Name of Company :

Subsidiaries:	Industry :

Phone Number :	Fax Number:

E-Mail Address/Other Phone Numbers :

Mailing Address :

Physical Address :

Group Administrator:	DOB	SS#
Executive Contact:	DOB	SS#
Other Contact:	DOB	SS#
Other Contact:	DOB	SS#
Other Contact:	DOB	SS#
Other Contact:	DOB	SS#
Other Contact:	DOB	SS#

HEALTH INSURANCE

Completed by:	Date:	Entered By:	Date:
Agent #1 ; %	Agent #2 ; %	Agent #3 ; %	Agent #4 ; %

Group #	Effective Date	Ann. Date

Carrier	Reinsurance Carrier (if applicable)

Name of PPO or HMO Network (if applicable)

Address To Send Claims

Carrier Contact Person	Number Enrolled

Employer Contribution	Individual	Individual/Child	Individual/Spouse	Family

IN NETWORK BENEFITS	OUT OF NETWORK BENEFITS
Deductible	Deductible
PCP Co-pay ; Specialist Co-pay	
Hospital Co-pay (If applicable)	
Coinsurance	Coinsurance
Maximum Out of Pocket (per Family)	Maximum Out of Pocket (per Family)
Generic Rx; Non Preferred Brand Rx;	Generic Rx ; Non Preferred Brand Rx;
Preferred Brand Rx; Drug Card Company:	Preferred Brand Rx; Drug Card Company:
Accident/Emergency Benefit	Accident/Emergency Benefit
Lifetime Maximum Benefit	Lifetime Maximum Benefit

Rates:	Individual	Individual/Child	Individual/Spouse	Family
1st of the Month Following…	☐ DOH	☐ 30 days ☐ 60 days	☐ 90 days ☒ other	

Other Benefits	Percentage

DENTAL INSURANCE

Completed by:	Date:	Entered By:	Date:
Agent #1 ; %	Agent #2 ; %	Agent #3 ; %	Agent #4 ; %

Group #	Effective Date	Ann. Date

Carrier

Address To Send Claims

Carrier Contact Person	Number Enrolled

Employer Contribution	Individual	Individual/Child	Individual/Spouse	Family

Dental Deductible	Deductible Applies to Coverages

Surgical Periodontics Covered?	Orthodontics Covered?	A, B, & C Maximum	D Lifetime Maximum

A Payment %	B Payment %	C Payment %	D Payment %

Rates:	Individual	Individual/Child	Individual/Spouse	Family
1st of the Month Following…	☐ DOH	☐ 30 days ☐ 60 days	☐ 90 days ☒ other	

Other Benefits	Percentage

LIFE INSURANCE

Completed by:		Date:		Entered By:			Date:		
Agent #1	; %	Agent #2	; %	Agent #3	;	%	Agent #4	;	%
Group #:			Effective Date:				Ann. Date :		
Carrier :									
Address To Send Claims :									
Carrier Contact Person :						Number Enrolled			
Life Schedule :				Classes:					
Rate Per $1,000 : Combined			Life			AD&D			
1st of the Month Following...	☐ DOH		☐ 30 days	☐ 60 days	☐ 90 days	☒ other			
Other Benefits:							Percentage		

SHORT TERM DISABILITY

Completed by:		Date:		Entered By:			Date:		
Agent #1	; %	Agent #2	; %	Agent #3	;	%	Agent #4	;	%
Group #:			Effective Date:				Anniversary Date :		
Carrier:									
Address To Send Claims:									
Carrier Contact Person:						Number Enrolled			
Duration of Benefits:	Weeks		0 Day Elimination Period for Accident			Day Elimination Period for Sickness			
Rate per $10 of Benefit:			% of Salary Benefit			$ Maximum Weekly Benefit			
1st of the Month Following...	☐ DOH		☐ 30 days	☐ 60 days	☐ 90 days	☒ other			
Other Benefits:							Percentage		
Plan Type : ☐ Voluntary	☒ Employer Paid	☐ Other							

LONG TERM DISABILITY

Completed by:		Date:		Entered By:			Date:		
Agent #1	; %	Agent #2	; %	Agent #3	;	%	Agent #4	;	%
Group #:			Effective Date:				Anniversary Date:		
Carrier :									
Address To Send Claims:									
Carrier Contact Person:						Number Enrolled:			
·Day Elimination Period			% of Salary Benefit			$ Maximum Monthly Benefit			
Rate per $100 of Covered Payroll:			Own Occupation Definition :						
1st of the Month Following...	☐ DOH		☒ 30 days	☐ 60 days	☐ 90 days	☒ other			
Other Benefits:							Percentage		
Plan Type : ☐ Voluntary	☒ Employer Paid	☐ Other							

SECTION 125

Completed by:		Date:		Entered By:			Date:		
Agent #1	; %	Agent #2	; %	Agent #3	;	%	Agent #4	;	%
Group # :			Effective Date:				Anniversary Date :		
Carrier :				Plan Type:					

COBRA/ HIPAA ADMINISTRATION

Completed by:		Date:		Entered By:			Date:		
Agent #1	; %	Agent #2	; %	Agent #3	;	%	Agent #4	;	%
Group #:			Effective Date:				Anniversary Date :		
Carrier :				Plan Type :					

DIRECTIONS:

CHAPTER

27

Employee Birthdays and Anniversaries

At The Hatcher Agency an employee's birth date and annual anniversary with the company are very important. Every time an employee has a birthday, we order a cake and everybody takes a little time out to celebrate with him or her in our lunchroom. We also do this for every annual anniversary the employee has with the company.

In addition to the little parties, we have anniversary date gifts. Listed below are our anniversary gifts for the first 10 years of employment:

First Year   Hatcher Agency Monogrammed Polo Shirt
Second Year   Lands End Monogrammed Gym Bag
Third Year   Mont Blanc Pen
Fourth Year   Lands End Monogrammed Round Duffel Bag
Fifth Year   Camera w/Zoom Lens
Sixth Year   Hatcher Agency Jean Button-down Shirt

Seventh Year	Hatcher Agency Windbreaker
Eighth Year	Highback Leather Office Chair
	(will be retained by the company)
Ninth Year	Hatcher Agency Sweat-suit or Hatcher Agency Robe
Tenth Year	19" Color TV w/VCR

Most of the anniversary gifts cost around $50 with a little bit more expensive gifts at five and ten years to show the significance of those anniversary dates.

This is one of the tools we use to let employees know how much we appreciate them and care about them as persons. It is also a good business practice. Ideas are a dime a dozen. People who put them into action are priceless. High turnover in personnel adversely affects the company, not only financially, but also in the quality of customer service. The little extras can be the reason an employee stays with the company. They can deliver the message that the employees are truly valued as the company's most important resource. Employees who do not feel appreciated will not deliver "Outrageous Service" to the clients. When we treat our employees like the special people they are, chances are they will treat the clients they service just as well.

You may wonder why an employee gets a high-back leather chair in the eighth year. There is a good reason. It was eight years after I started the company before I bought one for my office. I figure anyone who stays with us eight years deserves one too.

> *When you touch base with your clients*
> *on a regular basis, you show your*
> *dependability and build trust.*

CHAPTER

Fax Updates

At The Hatcher Agency, we send our clients a fax update once a month giving them information about what is going on regarding their account or the insurance carrier with which they are insured. We also send out weekly fax updates to clients that have a particular issue going on. Not every client gets a fax every week, but every account receives a minimum of one fax a month and may receive as many as four a month because we do weekly fax updates.

When dealing with a customer, there are some items that are better dealt with by sending a letter; others can be better handled with a phone call; some issues require making a visit in person; but there are some items that are dealt with more effectively with a fax update. Below are some examples of "fax items."

Let's say you have a person that is very difficult to get in touch with, but you have an appointment with that person for 9:00 a.m. tomorrow.

Sending a fax update to remind them that you will be coming to their office at 9:00 a.m. tomorrow is an effective way of getting the message across without having to play phone tag. The message is in writing so the receiver cannot misunderstand it.

Suppose you need to give directions to a client on how to get to your office. A fax update is much more effective than giving the information on the phone and having the person write down the directions, possibly making errors in the recording. Perhaps you want to touch base with a client to let them know that you have not forgotten them and that you are working on their project, but it is not completed. You just want them to know you are being conscientious and that you expect the project to be done in about three days.

Sometimes you have information you would like for a client to read, but you don't want to wait two days for the mail to deliver it. Again, a fax update can be quite effective. For items that are urgent, there is no better tool than the fax.

When faxes were a new concept, they were used to communicate urgent messages that needed to be delivered immediately upon receipt. In today's office environment most people still consider faxes urgent, and they are usually delivered to the addressee's desk immediately. In spite of the fact that virtually every office now has a fax machine and faxing is almost as commonplace as sending letters, businesses still tend to get those faxes to the right desk quickly and they are read immediately.

Fax updates are an important tool that everyone in your office can use to help deliver "Outrageous Service." Our fax updates serve as a goodwill tool to touch base with our clients on a weekly basis and give them information they need. Because sending out weekly fax updates is standard practice at our office, it serves as another tool that shows a commitment to customer service that very few of our competitors get around to using. You can make the fax update work for you in your business too.

When you touch base with your clients on a regular basis, you show your dependability and build trust.

NOTE: Following is a copy of a Fax Update that was sent to our clients to give you an idea.

THE
HATCHER
AGENCY

"Our Attitude is the Difference"

FAX UPDATE

TO: Marilyn Monroe	**FROM:** Greg Hatcher
COMPANY: ABC Company	**DATE:** June 3
FAX NUMBER: 555-1247	**FAX NUMBER:** 501-375-0446
PHONE NUMBER: 555-1246	**PHONE NUMBER:** 501-375-3737
RE: Form 5500 Filing	**TOTAL NUMBER OF PAGES INCLUDING COVER SHEET:** 1

URGENT	FOR REVIEW	PLEASE COMMENT	PLEASE REPLY	PLEASE RECYCLE

Now that tax season is in full swing and the IRS is on our mind, it is a good time to remind you about your Form 5500 filing. Following are some tips regarding the Form 5500 filing for Section 125 plans.

A **Form 5500** is filed for groups with 100 or more participants.
A **Form 5500 C/R** is filed for groups with fewer than 100 participants.

The Employee Retirement Income Security Act of 1974 (ERISA) Section 6039D requires that Form 5500 and **Schedule F** be completed by any employer that has a Section 125 Fringe Benefit Plan. These forms are filed with the Internal Revenue Service.

1. Schedule F and the Form 5500 are due by the end of the seventh month following the end of the Fringe Benefit Plan year. (Example: The Section 125 plan year ends January 31. The Schedule F is due by August 31 of that year.)

2. The employer should have the information necessary to complete the Schedule F.

3. In order to file this form with the IRS, they will need to complete Page 1 of the Form 5500 Annual Return, Lines 1a through 6d. In addition, Schedule F Lines 1 through 7.

4. The penalties for not filing this information with the IRS can be several thousand dollars, depending on the tardiness of the form and the amount of information missing.

   NOTES:

   For plans administered by FlexCo, they will contact the employer for the information each year and then complete the Schedule F and present it to the employer within 3 or 4 months following the end of the plan year. It is then the employer's responsibility to fill out the Form 5500 page 1 and file the forms with the IRS.

   For plans administered by CBS, they will provide the employer with any necessary information, and it is the employer's responsibility to complete and file the forms with the IRS.

   For plans administered by other companies, please check with that administrator to see what their practices are regarding Form 5500 filing.

Keep in mind that, in any case, filing the form is ultimately the *employer's responsibility.* Any penalties levied by the IRS will be the employer's responsibility to pay.

As always, give us a call if you have any questions or if we can help you in any way.

P.O. Box 3505 Little Rock, AR 72203 * Telephone (501) 375-3737 * 1-800-359-3748 * Fax (501) 375-0446

CHAPTER

29

A Dictation Unit is a Must

When I started the insurance agency, one of the most difficult things for me was writing a letter. It was almost impossible to sit down at my desk in the middle of the day, with employees interrupting and the phone ringing, and write a letter. It took a lot of time to hand write a letter on a note pad and then get it to my secretary to type.

When I complained to my father, the most organized man I have ever known, about the difficulty, he always told me buy a dictation unit and dictate my letters. He said the $30 hand-held unit and a unit for my secretary that would run about $200 would be the best $230 I would ever spend.

I told him over and over that I simply could not write a letter by talking into a recorder. I thought I had to write it down and read it over to be effective. He continued to tell me that if I would dictate the letter and let my secretary type it I could see it typed and could make any adjustments needed at that time. Still, I was stubborn and continued to write my letters and continued to complain. I probably complained to my father on ten different occasions, and each time he told me the dictation unit would solve my problems. He said he had felt the same way I did at one time but if I would just try dictating the letters, I would learn to write letters on a dictation unit as well as I could write them on paper.

My father was wrong. I soon learned that I could dictate letters a heck of a lot BETTER than I could write them on paper. The reasons are quite simple. When I dictate my letters, I generally dictate them where things are quiet—while I am driving in the car, when I am sitting in an airport, or when I am out of pocket where I am uninterrupted and all my thoughts can flow freely. There are no phone calls or employees, so I don't have to compose my letter in bits and pieces. I have learned that I can dictate a letter five times faster than I can write it. Imagine that. I can dictate five letters in the same period of time that I can write one! That time savings alone adds up to a tremendous increase in efficiency.

The fact that I dictate my letters when I am in the car immediately after leaving an appointment gives me such an advantage over my competitors that I consider the dictation unit one of the most important weapons in my "Outrageous Service" arsenal.

So what do I do with the time I save with my dictation machine? Well, for starters, I dictated this entire book. I never wrote one thing on a sheet of paper. I started with the table of contents and dictated the titles of chapters I wanted to write. When my secretary delivered the transcribed chapters, I would refer to the table of contents and dictate additional chapters. I dictated each chapter, reviewed the hard copy and made changes as needed. The entire book was dictated on vacations or long business trips. I would refer to my list of topics and dictate the chapters as I drove down the road. This is the only way I could write this book and still continue doing the day-to-day activities required by my job. Without the dictation unit, I would never have written this book.

Imagine what a difference it would make if after every appointment you got in the car and dictated a letter to your client following up on all the things you discussed and the items you needed done. Or, if you got in the car and dictated a list of the things your secretary needed to do for you. Or the items your service representative needed to take care of for that customer. Letters dictated immediately after an appointment can serve as valuable reminders of the service issues you need to take care of for that particular customer.

Some people use a dictation unit just to record important ideas and thoughts they have during the day and then have someone jot them down or type them. Others even type or write them themselves. A person who trusts his memory for all these things will be unorganized and inefficient because nobody's memory is perfect enough to remember all the things we think about each day. I have dictated three page lists of things I need to do on a house that I bought and am remodeling or things I needed to research before making the final offer.

Doctors may understand the importance of dictation better than anyone else. They see a patient and immediately dictate the specifics of the visit. The secretary types up the paragraph of notes and puts it in the file. This is how your doctor can remember what happened when he met with you last and what your symptoms and illnesses were. No doctor can remember 2,000 patients' medical histories and the details of each visit. If the doctor took the time to sit down and write all these things out on each patient, he would lose valuable time that he could spend seeing more patients each day. Why shouldn't you treat your clients with the same care and detail with which the doctor treats his patients?

Many large companies have dictation services that allow employees to call in 24 hours a day to dictate letters by telephone. The big company's word-processing department types the letters and delivers them to each person's desk the following day. What an effective way to help employees get their paperwork done at any hour of the day! The key to any efficient business is to have every employee doing what he or she does best. People who are best at typing letters type letters; people who are best at selling make sales, and people who are the best mechanics fix things. Having highly paid people write or type their own letters can cost the company a lot of money. If you have a $100,000-a-year employee typing letters when a $20,000 a-year-employee can get the job done more efficiently, you are wasting money. If you think you are busy right now and you don't have a dictation unit, run to the store and get one. It will save you countless hours and make you much more effective.

You can talk five times faster than you can write!

Birthday Cards

At the Hatcher Agency, we choose to be first, best, *and* different. Everybody likes to be remembered on birthdays. Some businesses don't send out birthday cards at all. Others send out a generic card with a printed message. A card with a personal message inside is a thousand times better.

At the Hatcher Agency, we go a step further and make our cards really special. We bake a birthday cake and have a party with all the staff dressed up in party hats. While we're celebrating the birthdays of all our customers and vendors, we have our picture taken. Then we have a card printed with the photo on the front and a message inside.

Last year's picture has our employees cramming into our Hatcher Agency van to "deliver" a happy birthday message. We have a new picture made and change the card on the same date each year, so nobody receives the same card twice. We are currently sending out over 150 birthday cards per month.

Our customers love these funny pictures with our employees all dressed up and acting crazy, and they will certainly never receive another card like it. Each member of our staff reviews our card list, so each employee knows when our clients' birthdays are. Before the cards go out, we write a little personal note on the inside of the card or the outside of the envelope.

We have a lot of fun making the birthday cards and entertaining our clients on their special day.

NOTE: On the following pages you will see photos of our last three years' birthday cards.

WISHING YOU A **WILD** AND **CRAZY**

BIRTHDAY FROM

THE HATCHER AGENCY

Leah Kirkland

Charla Reynolds

Sheen Ledbetter

Joyce White

Curtis Barely

Audrey Baker

Woody Hamel

Greg Hatcher

Barbara Steele

Barb Lust

Junior Ward

Jackie Martin

HAPPY BIRTHDAY

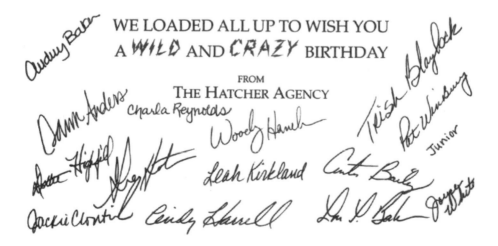

WE LOADED ALL UP TO WISH YOU
A *WILD* AND *CRAZY* BIRTHDAY

FROM
THE HATCHER AGENCY

HAPPY BIRTHDAY

Let the Kid in you show
on your Birthday,
we certainly did!

FROM
THE HATCHER AGENCY

PART THREE

"Outrageous Service" Ideas

> *There is nothing as frustrating*
> *or expensive as having to retrain*
> *a new person to be as good as*
> *the person that just left you.*

CHAPTER

31

You Cannot Deliver "Outrageous Service" with High Turnover

Because I began as a salesman in the insurance business, in my early years I thought the answer to any problem was to simply go out and sell more business. Nothing could be further from the truth. As our agency has grown, I have become as much an agency administrator as a salesman.

As an administrator I have learned that one of the most significant costs to any company is that of turnover and retraining new employees. There is nothing more frustrating than losing a good employee and then having to spend a ton of money and time to interview, hire and train someone up to the level of the person who left. It can take one to two years to get a new employee "up to snuff," especially in a business with as many details as insurance.

For any business—whether it is operating a gas station or making microcomputer chips—turnover is a hidden cost that many employers overlook. After losing several employees for various reasons in the early years of my business, I decided I was tired of turnover and was going to do everything I could to bring in the best people and retain them. My new strategy is a combination of things I had learned in two different areas.

The first education I got in regard to turnover had nothing to do with the insurance business. I had a house I had rented out for quite some time. When I first started renting the house, I tried to charge a rate that was aggressive and would bring a good profit. I found that I could get renters in, but they would find a better deal. Then they would give notice, and I would have to start over and find a new renter. I had to go through their credit history, repaint the walls, and make some changes to customize the house to the needs of the new renters. Generally I was a month or two without rent. I learned that one or two months' lost rent ate up a full year or even two years, of the additional profit I made by charging an aggressive rate.

I looked at the house I was renting and found that comparable houses in the area were renting for $800 a month. So I rent mine for $700. I interview candidates who want to rent the house, and they know from shopping the market that this house is $100 below the market. I tell them I will rent them the house for $700, and will not increase the rent if they take care of the little details on the house and keep it in good shape. If the water heater breaks or the back door needs adjusting, they can call and make arrangements to have the repairs done and send me the bill. If the bill is going to exceed $200, they are to call and let me give prior approval. They will make arrangements with the plumber or other technicians and have someone there to let them in. If the renters keep their agreement, I will give them a better rent rate without increases.

This approach puts the renter and me on the same team and with the same goal. We want the house to run smoothly with as little hassle as possible for both of us. Traditional renters charge aggressive rates, but when something goes wrong, they have to call around to get someone to fix it. They have to go out and arrange a time to get the key and go through the entire hassle associated with repairs. I have found that when I give my renter a better than average deal, the renter stays in the house, is happy with the deal and feels he has control of the situation. The renter that is currently in my house has lived there for over three years without a rent increase, and I have dropped by to visit him one time just to make a goodwill check. The fact that I have low turnover on this house has saved me a lot of money.

In America everyone wants a bargain. When most companies hire someone for a certain position, they try to spend the least amount of money possible to fill that position. A book I read encouraged employers to try just one time to fill the next open position by recruiting the very best employee they could find and pay the person the highest salary the company could afford for that position. I decided to try this philosophy. I hired my first employee under this premise about five years after I was in business, and I have never hired an employee under any other premise since.

Assume you are hiring a receptionist, and the going rate for the position is $18,000 a year. If you interview well and are willing to pay a receptionist $20,000 a year, you will get the best receptionist on the market. The receptionist will not be constantly looking for other jobs where she can make a little more money. As long as you and the receptionist understand that she is making more than the going rate and you provide the other important factors such as good working conditions, respect and a job she can take pride in, you can keep that receptionist. I have found since we adopted this policy that we only lose employees when spouses get transferred, employees retire, or they decide to make a complete industry change.

Of course, salary is not the only consideration in keeping good employees. We also provide a pleasant working environment with private offices and good benefits, and we are generous in regard to personal days, sick pay and other benefits.

The fact that we have been able to reduce our turnover and hire better people by paying just a little bit more has been one of the best moves our company ever made. Our employees don't leave our company to go to work for our competitors.

It is impossible to deliver great service to the client when you constantly have new people coming in who do not know the ins and outs of the business and are not familiar with the clients. Turnover will always be a part of your business, but if you can keep your turnover to less than ten percent, you are doing an outstanding job. This means that at least 90 percent of the employees your clients are working with are people who are familiar with their accounts. Ten percent turnover as opposed to a rate of 25 percent can make a huge difference in your company's bottom line, the morale of your employees, and the service your customers receive.

One big advantage of paying our employees a little more is that it makes me feel good. The fact that we have a bunch of All-Stars on our team who are well paid has done a lot for my self esteem and pride in our company. It also does a great deal for our entire staff. Everybody wants to work for a winner, and I now find it easier to recruit and get more winners. A part of every interview process we have at The Hatcher Agency involves the candidate going around and talking with three or four of our employees for fifteen minutes and letting them tell him or her what it is like to work for me and The Hatcher Agency. Our employees sell a prospective employee on coming to work at The Hatcher Agency. We feel our company is a great place to work, and we want anyone who joins us to feel the same way.

Give your employees a good deal and keep them happy. They will stay with the company a long time and that will make the customers happy. Everybody wins.

CHAPTER

32

You Have Made A Mistake That Hurts A Customer . . . Now What?

Sometimes a business makes a mistake, and the customer gets the short end of the deal. When this happens, it is important to see the mistake as an opportunity to improve your relationship with your customer. All companies make mistakes; many companies spend a lot of time regretting mistakes; and a few companies are creative enough to find ways to turn a mistake into something positive for the customer.

We have all gone through a drive-thru window at a fast food restaurant, given our order, and driven off to find that our hamburger or french fries are missing, the special sauce we want is not in the bag, or we were given the wrong drink. Some of us have turned around and gone back to the establishment to get our order correct although we were inconvenienced by having to get in the line again. When the fast food establishment corrects our order and we leave, we still do not feel happy about the service we received. The bottom line is that we were inconvenienced and we wish they had prepared the order right the first time.

If the restaurant had apologized, given us our food for free, or even given us a coupon for a free meal, we would have gone away with a totally different impression of that company. We all realize that people make mistakes, and most of us are willing to overlook an occasional error. But, when the company that makes a mistake takes care of you in such a way that compensates you for the trouble, you feel a lot better about the error.

Suppose you go to a restaurant where you made reservations. They forgot to reserve your table, and you have a long wait. A creative head-waiter that served you free drinks while you waited could go a long way toward helping you forget the mistake and restoring your confidence in the restaurant.

When we make a mistake in the insurance business, we try to correct it financially and then do something to make up for the customer's inconvenience. We try to leave the customer feeling that things are better than they were before the error was made.

The creative company that can make things better when a mistake has been made will not only retain the customer but will improve the relationship. Furthermore, the customer will tell the story of how the company took care of him when things went wrong, and people who hear the story will want to do business with that company. Everybody likes to feel listened to, and a company's decision to correct a mistake in a creative way can make the customer feel very powerful and important.

Obviously, your goal as a company is to avoid making mistakes because mistakes cost money. If you handle the mistake wrong, it will cost you more money and possibly cause you to lose the customer for life. Merely correcting the mistake costs extra time, and you may still lose the customer. If you correct the mistake in such a way that the customer comes out ahead, it costs you more in the short run; but keeping that customer is a lot more valuable in the long haul.

There are some mistakes that simply cannot be compensated for. If an airline runs three hours late and you miss a special event with your son or daughter, nothing can correct that. However, complimentary tickets can sure make things better. People know when companies are trying to take care of them, and in the end that is what matters. It is a simple philosophy and a simple solution. When you have made a mistake, own up to it and fix it so that your customer gains more than he lost, and your organization will prosper.

> *No matter what anyone says,*
> *everyone works a little harder*
> *when an incentive is attached.*

CHAPTER

33

Administrative Bonuses
for All Employees

Whatever happened to the employee who worked with a sense of pride in seeing a job well done? In an ideal world, we all do a good job because it is the right thing to do. My experience in the real world tells me that we are all human, and we all have selfish and lazy tendencies. If you want to make sure something gets done in your organization, tie some incentives to it. We all have goals that we want to accomplish, but we can get the job done better and more promptly when there is an incentive on the line.

To prove my theory that administrative bonuses can make your organization work better, let me give you a couple of examples of things I was never able to achieve without an administrative bonus. When I started the agency, I asked our employees to write five thank you notes a week to people who had done a good job for them—a vendor, customer or just anyone they had worked with that week. Each week I asked who wrote their five thank you notes and, much to my chagrin, most of the time fewer than half the staff had gotten around to writing thank you notes. I preached and preached about how important thank you notes are and how they can help develop better relationships for us. Each week at staff meeting I got the same result. I could not get the staff to write the notes on a consistent basis. Finally, because I believed so strongly in the policy, I implemented a bonus system. If people wrote five thank you notes or more per week and turned in a list by the first of each month of the names of the people and their relationship to the company, they would receive a $50 administrative bonus. As you might expect, my staff was 100 percent effective. The next month every employee wrote the notes and turned in the list.

Bonuses also helped us achieve a long-standing request to make monthly goodwill calls to our clients. My first year in business, I wanted each service representative to call each client just to check in and make sure we were giving the service they needed. I asked them to turn in reports to me each month with a little paragraph on how things were going with each of their accounts. Again, I could never get the reports in on a regular basis; and if I did get them, almost never had the service representative contacted every group. I begged and preached the importance of this and insisted that I absolutely had to have the reports each month. Finally, after four or five months of not getting the results I wanted, I let everybody know that I would pay a $100 bonus if I got the goodwill call reports on my desk by the first of each month. Shazam! We now have 100 percent compliance. Every employee turned in a complete report.

It sounds as though administrative bonuses are given to employees who don't do their job correctly, so we are rewarding them for doing the job they were hired to do in the first place. I admit I felt that way myself until I realized that we could deduct the amount of administrative bonuses from the basic salary we offered new employees. They would still get all the salary allotted for the job, but they would earn part of it when they wrote thank you notes and made goodwill calls. Now part of every employee's salary is tied to job performance. These incentives allow me to tell employees one time what is necessary and no longer spend time reminding them to get these tasks done.

Administrative bonuses should be tied to important administrative tasks that are extremely hard to get people to do on a regular basis. Every organization has some of these tasks. Every person in our organization has at least one task that is tied to an administrative bonus. My office manager's bonus is tied to getting our commission audit done on time each month. Prior to the bonus formula, we were three and four months behind on our commission audit. The office manager also gets a bonus for getting commissions out to our agents by the fifteenth of each month. Prior to the bonus policy, we consistently delivered these checks from the 24th to the 30th of the month. Once employees know they get their bonus only if the work is done on time, all excuses are eliminated.

I recently read an article on the NBA playoffs about why it is so difficult for a team to repeat as champions. After a team wins a championship, the media often asks them whether they expect to win the title again. Their answers are often like, "Well, if we have some good luck, if we don't have any major injuries, if we can get everybody back again, we can win another championship." In other words, the team was not willing to make the commitment: "Yes, we will absolutely repeat as champions, and we will do whatever it takes to meet that goal."

If you tell employees that the deadline is the fifteenth unless a little something goes wrong, something will go wrong. In business nothing ever goes right all the time. This is why bonuses are so important. Bonuses eliminate excuses and get employees to meet their goals ahead of time so that if something does go wrong, they will still meet the deadline. Place administrative bonuses on the items that are essential for outrageous service to the customer. Certainly, you cannot tie a bonus to every single item, but you will be amazed at how many items you can tie them to.

Staff Meeting
at 7:00 a.m.

How often have you called a company to ask to speak to someone and were told that person is in a meeting? You then ask for the assistant and learn that that person is also in a meeting. You ask to speak with any customer representative and find that all of them are in a meeting. It becomes obvious that this company is having a staff meeting during the business day at a time when you need service.

Most companies have their staff meetings during the business day, which means service for the customer is shut down. We constantly impress on our staff that customers do not care about our staff meeting or our vacation or the fact that our child is sick today. They care about getting the services they are paying for. For this reason, we always have our staff meetings on Tuesday morning at 7:00 a.m. The reason we have them so early is that we want to meet when it is convenient for our customer instead of when it is convenient for ourselves.

We have learned, however, that it is actually convenient for our staff to have a meeting at 7:00 a.m. At that time, we can all concentrate on getting the issues at hand resolved without the phone ringing off the hook and being interrupted by emergencies that may occur during a staff meeting held during business hours.

When we hire someone we let him or her know about our 7:00 a.m. commitment. We videotape all our staff meetings for employees who are sick or out of town on the day we have the meeting. This way they can come back and watch the video and we don't have to repeat ourselves or pass on fragmented information from the meeting.

Having our staff meeting early allows us to get more done in that one hour because we have no interruptions. We can also get more done for our customers when the workday begins at 8:00 a.m. These early morning weekly meetings are a commitment that allows us to give a full workweek to our customers.

One final note in regard to the early morning meeting. Several people have said, "Boy, I would not want to go to work for a company that had meetings at such a ridiculous hour." People have told me that my employees would not stand for the early meetings. As a former high school and college athlete, the coaches I remember best and the teams I enjoyed playing for most were the ones that were the most demanding. The coach that pushed me a little harder and the team that had higher standards and the hardest work ethics were the teams I was most proud to play on. They were also the teams that won the most games. I have found that my employees are actually proud of the fact that we have a 7:00 a.m. meeting.

They may not enjoy getting up when the alarm clock goes off, but they like the once-a-week meeting without interruptions. I have actually heard employees boast to friends, customers and family that we have our staff meetings at 7:00 a.m. They are proud of the fact that they have made that commitment to the customer. Everyone feels good about working a little harder to do a good job whether it is at work, in a classroom, or on the sports field. I think our 7:00 a.m. meetings help give our employees a champion's attitude.

35

Hatcher Time

(The Hatcher Agency On-Time Rules)

As you know from the previous chapter, we have all of our 23 employees meet at 7:00 a.m. for staff meeting. We have our staff meetings at this time so we will not all be in a meeting when a customer calls in for service. As you may know, getting 23 people to be anywhere on time is a chore. Trying to have them at work and ready to go at 7:00 a.m. is a real challenge.

There are a few situations, however, where people tend to be on time. The common denominator that is required in getting people anywhere on time is a drop-dead deadline. For example, the airline does not care why you are five minutes late. If you are five minutes late, the plane will take off without you no matter who you are. Think about all of the professional sporting events that take place every day in America. How often is somebody absent from the starting lineup because he was late? Having a business that runs on time requires the same kind of drop-dead deadlines. Any manager that has ever run a meeting with a substantial number of employees knows how frustrating it is to get them all there by start time. I know of managers who lock the door at the set time when they have their staff meeting. If people are not there on time, they are shut out of the meeting because managers feel it is not fair for the prompt employees to have to wait for five or ten minutes for everyone to get there so things don't have to be repeated.

I dealt with this frustration for several years at The Hatcher Agency. I still have to deal with it when I coach sports teams and work in civic organizations. The difference at The Hatcher Agency is that I pay employees to be there on time, so I can set tough standards to live by. All Hatcher Agency employees set their watches fifteen minutes prior to the hour. Setting our watches a little bit ahead provides an immediate panic alert that makes us feel our deadline is closer than it actually is. I made a decision after getting upset at several staff meetings because I had to repeat myself or have 20 employees at high dollar wages sit and wait for ten minutes for someone to arrive, that we would start at 7:00 a.m. with or without them. When I walk into staff meeting at 7:00 a.m. sharp everybody should already be in their seats with their coffee and pens and papers, having eliminated every possible reason for delaying our staff meeting. Setting these guidelines up front reminds everybody to arrive at the office fifteen minutes prior to 7:00 a.m. so they will not be rushing at a mad sprint to get to the meeting on time.

The problem with people being on time is that if they are trying to arrive somewhere at 7:00 a.m., they often fail to allow for a margin of error. If I am going to be somewhere at 7:00, I give myself ten to fifteen minutes for things to go wrong. The extra time allows me to be calm and avoid all the stress of getting there at the last minute. If a little something goes wrong along the way, I have a few minutes to spare and can still be there on time. If everything goes as planned and I arrive at my client's office fifteen minutes early, I may sit in the car, get my thoughts together, do some other organizational items, and walk in precisely on time.

My father was a great business trainer for me, and I asked him how many minutes early I should be for an appointment. His answer was, "You should not arrive substantially early or substantially late; you should be right on time." The key is to get to the appointment a few minutes early and then walk in the office a minute or two prior to your appointment time. All of us understand what it is like to have to stop what we are doing to visit with someone who shows up 30 minutes early for an appointment. We don't want to inconvenience them, but their arriving early may wreak havoc with our planned day. If you do arrive early and have no place to wait other than at the client's office, let the receptionist know that you realize you are early and do not want to inconvenience the client. Make it known that you do not mind waiting 30 minutes; but if the client wants to meet with you early, you can certainly do that. Many of us have heard the old saying, "Ninety percent of success is showing up." Another quote might be that "Ninety-five percent of success is showing up on time." I am convinced that showing up on time tells clients they can depend on you.

All members of our staff know that if they are going to be even one minute late getting to the client's office, they should call on the car phone to let the client know they are running a minute late but are on the way. Certainly, it is best not to be late to begin with, but if you are going to be the least bit late, you can avoid inconveniencing your client further by calling. This courtesy will also show the client that you pay attention to details and will always be considerate of their time as you service the account.

I have always liked to play the percentage game, and I believe that being on time and prepared will significantly increase my chances for making a sale. Fortunately, these are two criteria I can generally control very well.

Hatcher Agency employees don't say, "Oh I'm late for everything. I am chronically late. I do better under pressure." Our people can be depended on to get up early enough to have a few minutes to spare and not spend their life in a mad rush. If you follow this policy, you will be amazed at how much better your day goes and how much more successful you will be.

NOTE: When I was dictating this chapter, one of our staff members laughed and said it is really quite funny to work at The Hatcher Agency because if someone asks what time it is they have to ask, "Do you want real time or Hatcher time?" This is how focused and oriented all the employees are to the difference between running their lives fifteen minutes early and running exactly on time.

Be a List Maker

Statistics show that people who make lists of things to do each day make more than twice as much money as those who do not make lists. People who begin each day by organizing a list of things to do and checking them off as they finish each task get a lot more done than those who walk into the day without a plan. We have all heard from speakers in seminars and on TV that people who have written goals achieve more than people who don't. In spite of these facts, many people don't take time to set these goals and do their "To Do" lists.

Business is one of the easiest areas to be successful in. You don't have to be born with a lot of money; you don't have to be 6 feet, 10 inches tall; you don't have to be great looking or in great physical shape. You do have to be organized, and the best way to do that is to make a "To Do" list each day and follow it. Accomplishing your list of goals each day won't guarantee that you will be Bill Gates and own Microsoft, but it will help you get organized, and will add to your incentive to show up on time and work hard. If you do these things, you will excel.

I always wanted to be a professional athlete. To be a professional athlete you have to have some God-given talents in addition to a great work ethic and a lot of discipline. To be great in business you can eliminate the need to be able to run a 4.4-second 40-yard dash or to have a 42-inch vertical jump or to be 6 feet 6 inches tall. To be a business success you need things like a big heart, a good work ethic and the discipline to plug away and do the little things you need to do each day to get the job done. One of these "little things" is making lists. Regardless of the business you are in, you will be more successful if you are a list maker.

Who do you need to call today? What do you need to get done for each client? To whom do you need to write a note? What meetings do you have scheduled? What reading do you need to do? What personal business do you need to take care of? When will you exercise? Plan your day. Make a list. When planning your day, all business, personal, and family items should be coordinated into one list for a total plan. Check each item off as you accomplish that task. At the end of the day, check again to make sure you have covered everything. You will be amazed at how much more you will get done.

Write It Down

Nothing makes me doubt people's intentions and the ability to get a job done for me more than the fact that they don't write down what I tell them. I sometimes bring in contractors to work on my house and may show them fifteen or twenty things I want done, with details on each item. Many times these contractors just sit there and nod. They do not have their pencil and paper out writing down my instructions. It absolutely drives me crazy. I generally get out a pencil and paper or type up a list for them and give it to them.

Certain industries are notorious for feeling that they have great memories, but I am convinced that "writing it down" will improve any industry's performance. Even the employee with a "perfect memory" would do well to write down the customer's requests. This sends the message that the employee understands what the customer wants and intends to get the job done.

At The Hatcher Agency we teach all employees to have pen and paper ready when they call on a client. When the customer makes a request, they are to write it down. That way, they can remember what it was they wanted to get done, and the customer feels they've been heard and the representative will take care of the details. When the customer requests several items they need our agency to do for them, we run back over the list just before we end the meeting and confirm that these are the things that need to be done. Sometimes when the list is read back, the customer will think of one or two other items to add to the list.

On big issues or projects, it is a good idea to follow up a meeting with a letter listing all the items we will be working on, especially if there are things that will not be taken care of immediately. If there are items the client is responsible for, we list those in the letter also. The letter can serve as a record and a reminder for both parties. Communication is crucial in business. If you can understand what the customer wants you to do and communicate all the elements to the people working on various projects, you can get the job done and always stay a leg up on the competition.

All too often people spend hundreds of hours working on a project only to find that there was a misunderstanding on exactly what needed to be done. Writing things down and clearly communicating verbally and in writing what the client wants is critical to success.

My belief in "writing it down" is so strong that if an employee doesn't write it down when I make a request, I pull out an 8½" x 11" sheet of paper and hand it to them as a reminder. We don't make notes on little sticky notes or odd sheets of paper. We use only 8½" x 11" paper so we don't have some little scrap that gets lost among the shuffle with larger pages or in a file folder.

We also find that if we write even a little note on a full sheet of paper, when the request is completed, we can give that paper back or write a response to the person we are working with. We don't waste a lot of paper; we recycle letters, memos and proposals from our insurance carriers by turning them over and using the backs for internal communication. The practice of everybody writing it down on 8½" x 11" paper gives our company system wide organization and communication.

CHAPTER

How About a
Personal Coach?

Everyone understands the concept of a personal trainer today. The personal trainer helps you to get your body in shape and improve your overall physical strength. When you are physically strong and healthy, you can be a better parent, do better in your weekend warrior sports activities and yes, even do a better job at work.

But, physical strength is not enough. Emotional well-being is as important as physical health in dealing with the stress of life—juggling multiple commitments to home and family, the community, and work.

Most employees have a manager they can turn to for support. But, each company has a person at the top—the President, the CEO or the business owner—whose job it is to have the vision for the company. That person really has no one he can talk to or share his dreams with and work out that vision. Some business owners discuss their employee problems, issues in their personal lives or company financial problems with another employee. Discussing these sensitive issues may cause erosion of trust as that employee wonders whether you are talking about him with someone else. So where does the owner go with sensitive issues and personal problems that need to be kept private? A personal coach in this area can be as effective as a personal physical trainer.

As the President, CEO and owner of The Hatcher Agency, I have a personal coach, a person I see once a week to discuss the trials and tribulations of my business. My personal coach is a unique individual who has a Christian background and is a licensed counselor. He has counseled many individuals through marital problems, relationships with children and elderly parents, coping with the death of a loved one and dealing with terminal illness. My personal coach has been through all the experiences of life through his clients, and the fact that he has owned his own business for many years makes him a good person to talk to.

Depending on the week, he is my mentor, my sounding board, my priest, my friend and my financial advisor. Although he does give me good advice from time to time, the fact that I can "let it all out" to him releases a lot of stress for me and prevents my doing damage by saying things that need not be said to employees, family members, or others. Very few business owners take one hour a week to sit down and talk about the week, strategize and get feedback from a good business counselor. Most business owners are lucky to be able to do this two or three times a year. The fact that I am able to do it 52 times a year has made a big difference to me.

My personal coach is a third party that helps me a great deal with issues in raising my children, hiring a new employee, being a better husband or focusing on what the real issues are and what are the most important things in life.

A personal coach is not expensive. You may have a person who is willing to do it for free, or you may get a professional mentor that you can pay anywhere from $50 to $150 a session to work with you. Choosing your mentor is extremely important as you are going to share your innermost secrets with this person and count on him or her for advice on the most important issues in your life. You certainly need a person you can respect and trust to keep your discussions confidential. A psychologist, a psychiatrist, a social worker or even an older retired executive may love the opportunity to serve as a personal coach and help build you up mentally and spiritually to be the very best you can be. The rewards are not just for you, but for your personal coach as well as he or she takes a lot of satisfaction in helping you become your very best.

You may think that you are one of those people who are your own man or woman and you do not need anyone to help you. To some degree, even Michael Jordan has a personal coach. Since his father died, he has an older gentleman that goes everywhere with him. He serves as Michael's father, bodyguard, and mentor and is a person he can turn to for advice. No matter who you are, no matter how successful you are, you can be happier and more successful with a personal coach. A personal coach is a must for the business owner with all his responsibilities in life, but a personal coach can help each and every person with the struggles they have to deal with in everyday life. Life seems to get more complex every day. When both members of a couple work outside the home, the challenge of going to work, spending time with the children, getting dinner on the table, staying in shape, getting the next promotion and paying all the bills is more than virtually any normal human can handle easily. As you struggle through the issues that all of us must deal with, the personal coach can make a big difference.

CHAPTER

39

Seek First to Understand ...
Then to be Understood

The biggest mistake I made in my early years in management was to jump to conclusions when problems occurred with employees, insurance carriers, and anybody that I came in contact with. It is funny as we age how we learn not to jump to conclusions quite so quickly and to make sure we gather all the facts before we make a final decision. I have learned to sleep on things, to give it a week before I make a very important decision, and to let things settle in my mind.

Some of my very favorite people in the world are men and women over 65 years old. As I write this book at age 37, I feel like I have miles and miles to go before I will be as wise as these individuals. One of the reasons is that there is no shortcut for experience and tenure. Older people seem to be more accepting and tolerant of others and they are better listeners. These individuals have lived long enough to endure a lot of the ups and downs of life. They have seen just about everything happen both in their own lives and with other people. They are not shocked and amazed quite as easily, and they are not quick to over react.

When I was growing up, my father always told me about all the things I needed to be concerned about in life—such as drugs, gambling, sex, dishonesty, driving while intoxicated, spousal abuse, child abuse, etc. At sixteen, seventeen, and eighteen years old I thought my father was a hypochondriac and a worrier. It is only over the last nineteen years that I have realized that some of my friends did die in car accidents, and I now know people who have gambling and sexual addiction problems. I know people who went to jail for embezzlement. I have known people who committed suicide—and all the other things my father warned me about. The difference is that when I was sixteen years old, I had not lived long enough to see all the struggles in life.

One of the things I have learned as a manager is to listen to the other person's perspective before I give my side of the story. This works well with employees, customers, a spouse, friends, and anyone else you deal with. Generally when there is a conflict, each person wants to get his point across first and convince the other side that his way is right. However, if you can be willing to listen first to the other person's perspective, take it all in, and then get your point across, you will immediately become more successful in your relations with other people.

I attended a seminar with Stephen Covey, one of the best motivational speakers in the country. In his seminar he said to "Seek First To Understand, Then To Be Understood." I have found this a good principal to live by. If you try to understand the other person's perspective, you may see his side of the story and agree, thus avoiding conflict. Even if you don't agree with his side of the story, the very fact that you listened and let him air out his concerns will make him a lot more willing to listen to you and in the end improve your chances of working out a winnable solution.

How many times have you jumped to a conclusion and jumped on somebody's case only to find out he was late or something went wrong because there was a death in the family or some other situation that was totally out of his control? You felt like you stuck your foot in your mouth and hurt the relationship. Have you ever chewed some-one out and had him or her sit patiently until you finished and then give you a short distinct answer that made it very clear that he was not in the wrong? You wasted all this time destroying your credibility. Seeking first to understand and then to be understood will help you in all your relationships. Implement the principle in your personal life and in your business life, and you will find that you will be better at the most important skill in business: communicating effectively with other people.

PART FOUR

"Outrageous Service"
Equals Outrageous Sales

Incentives Must Be Service-Based to Ensure Great Service

I know a company that pays its salespeople nine times more to sell to a new client than to keep a client. The message here is simple: You can lose eight clients and sell one new one and still be better off.

The company pays the sales staff to focus on new sales and assumes the business will stay on the books once it is sold. Although most of the business will stay with the company, there are representatives who will smile when a piece of business is lost. They know they will have a chance to get the business again and receive nine times the income they would have received for keeping it. When I started The Hatcher Agency, I was determined to make sure that our company incentives were based first and foremost on keeping the business we had and then on selling new business.

As we discussed earlier, keeping employee turnover low saves money and helps your company deliver better service. The same principle applies to customer turnover. Keeping the customers you have is a lot less expensive than finding new customers and convincing them that the service you deliver is great while you are losing a customer out the back door. Over the years I have tried different incentives with employees, and the formula that has worked best for us is a net-gain incentive. We provide incentives to add new business in our company just like all others do. However, if an agent adds 100 new clients and loses 100 existing clients, then the incentive pay is zero. Incentive pay is based on net customer gain.

When we first started this incentive, if a company went out of business or was purchased and merged in a corporate buy-out, this loss did not count against the net-gain incentive. I later changed the incentive plan to be very straightforward and as simple as possible. Regardless of why we gain or lose a client, the bottom line is the net gain. All our employees are paid on net gain for clients.

I have found with the new incentive that our employees fight a little harder during that corporate takeover to become the agent for the new company. Our representatives are a lot more interested in getting coverage for our companies who have purchased other smaller companies and getting these employees added to the policies. And, when a company goes out of business, our employees tend to find a way to write coverage on the few employees that start their own companies. The bottom line in any business is to give people an incentive to do what will make your company stronger. If you don't give them the same incentives for keeping old business that you give for bringing in new business, you will have high turnover in your customer base. New business is good and necessary, but it costs more than renewed business. If you give employees incentives to keep the business you have on the books first and provide great customer service, you will maintain your customer base and get new customer referrals because of your reputation.

We also have lots of incentives to help keep operating costs down. One example we have is that if employees make a premium calculation error, or if they have to overnight mail something to a client, 50 percent of the cost for the error comes out of their incentive pay. It doesn't matter why we have to overnight the package or why a premium calculation error was made, it costs them 50 percent because it costs our company money that could have been used to help us deliver "Outrageous Service" to our customers. Last year we only had four packages that had to be mailed overnight. I know of other companies that overnight items routinely because there is no incentive for employees to help keep costs down. My philosophy is that if we have to overnight something, we have not done our job well because we did not anticipate the service the customer would need. We have a full-time courier that eliminates a great deal of the need for overnight mailing. Overnight mail is one of the most important innovations in business and is a product I am endeared to. But, I only want to overnight items that truly need to be sent overnight, and our incentive works.

You may think if you make the employee pay 50 percent of the overnight mail charge, employees will fail to deliver great service rather than have their pay reduced. This is not true for us because failing to overnight could mean an even greater loss to our employee—the possible loss of a client. Every employee must think and make decisions as if he or she was a business owner spending his or her own money instead of the company's money.

When employees know that calculations on premium errors could cost them money, they do a lot better job of quoting prices correctly to prospective clients. The carrots you provide for your employees need to be geared toward getting customers the service they need and keeping the business on the books. This focus on renewing the business we have has helped keep our clients happy, earned us almost 100 percent of our business by referral and made everybody happier in the process.

> *"It is a greater honor to teach*
> *someone else to be the best*
> *than to be the best yourself."*
> *— Dan Gable,*
> *former wrestling coach,*
> *University of Iowa,*
> *15 National Championships*

The Dan Gable Story

We all learn lessons in life in different ways. I learned a lot of valuable lessons as a high school and college wrestler. Wrestling is one of the most demanding sports that anyone could ever participate in. It requires being in tip-top physical shape, cutting weight, and being forced to perform one on one against your opponent in front of a lot of people. When you are finished, you come off the mat with no excuses. There are no teammates to blame; it is simply you against your opponent. I won a lot of wrestling matches, and I lost a lot of wrestling matches; but wrestling taught me how to have the courage to enter the battle and be able to win gracefully or lose knowing that I gave my maximum effort. I learned that losing when giving your maximum effort is nothing to be ashamed of.

Dan Gable is the greatest wrestler in the history of the sport. As a high school wrestler, he won three consecutive state titles and never lost a single match (freshman were not eligible then). He went on to Iowa State University and won every match of his college career except the last one. He won national championships his sophomore and junior years with undefeated records. His senior year, he lost in the National Championship Finals. He later went on to wrestle in the Olympics and did not allow one point during the entire Olympic Meet, winning the gold medal. Dan Gable's wrestling career was quite astonishing. He had a wrestling room in his home and trained harder than any wrestler ever to compete in the sport. In fact, Gannett News Service recently voted him the top wrestler of the *century*!

Dan Gable recently retired as the wrestling coach for the University of Iowa. When asked which he enjoyed more, being the wrestler or the coach, I was struck by his response. He said it was a greater honor to be able to teach someone to be the best than to be the best himself. Dan Gable won only two national championships as a wrestler, but as a coach he coached over 150 All-Americans and led Iowa to fifteen team National Wrestling Championships. Translated into business, this says you are more valuable to your company if you can teach other people to be the best in their professions than if you try to do it all yourself. As a sales manager, president, or leader in any department within your company, your most valuable asset is to be able to teach others to be their very best as Dan Gable did. We often try to do it all ourselves or put the most value on the one person who is the superstar, but the most valuable person to your organization is the one that can lead others to the promised land of success.

Of course, it always helps to lead by example. Dan Gable earned a lot of respect as a wrestler before he became a teacher. Although success on your own is generally a prerequisite to becoming a good coach, there are exceptions. There are some people who are great players but could never be great coaches, and there are many that are great coaches that would never be great players. The key is to develop both players and coaches in your organization, and you will have a winning team.

CHAPTER

"Outrageous Service" Will Get You Referrals

From the movie, "The Field Of Dreams," came the famous saying, "If you build it, they will come." Most people would interpret that to mean that if you build a great product, people will come to buy it. While this is certainly true, it is also true that if you give your customers Outrageous Service, they will tell others and you will get referrals. I find it strange that in the insurance business and other businesses there are so many people advertising gimmicks on ways to get referrals from your clients without their knowing they are giving them. These methods may be effective, but there is a better way to get prospects. Instead of asking your clients for the names of their accountants, lawyers, and friends, why not just earn your referrals?

From the beginning I knew I did not want to spend a lot of dollars on advertising. I didn't want to buy mailing lists to generate leads or spend countless hours on the phone, calling people who did not know who I was and didn't want to talk to me. So I decided to deliver service that would be so outstanding and so outrageous that it would naturally generate referrals without my even having to ask. After all, an unsolicited referral is the most valuable one you can have. Just as you can be sure that customers will go out and tell friends when they receive poor service from a company, you can also be sure that they will tell friends if you deliver outstanding service. Customers receive "Outrageous Service" so rarely and are so pleased when they do that they want to share the good news about your business. In order to get your clients to tell the whole world about your service, you have to deliver more than the usual, standard or normal. It must simply be "Outrageous."

How do you deliver "Outrageous Service?" It is not necessarily one thing you do, but a combination of everything you do when dealing with a client that adds up to this "Outrageous Service." At our agency it starts from the very beginning. When our clients call, the phone is answered by a person who works hard to connect them to another person rather than to voice mail. Once we get the referred client in, we write a thank-you note to the person who referred them. We tell them the contact has been made and report on the status of the referral. This lets them know that we appreciate and notice the effort they are giving us and that earns us more referrals in the future.

We contact referrals immediately and send them a letter following our phone visit to let them know what we will be working on for them and to confirm our meeting time. This letter goes out immediately with information on the special features and the "Outrageous Service" our agency delivers. If we visit the client in the morning, we have donuts with us; if it is in the afternoon, we have cookies. This gives the prospect a quick sense that we appreciate the opportunity to do business with them and want to have a friendly meeting. After meeting with the client, follow up is always swift. If they purchase a policy, we go out and enroll them in person and deliver their policies, insurance identification cards, and other information later in person. After the client is on the books, we call them every single month on a goodwill call just to see how they are doing and to keep them informed of what is going on in the business. These goodwill calls are absolutely unheard of in the insurance business; almost nobody checks with their clients each month to see how they are doing. Most agencies are generally out trying to sell new policies, meeting with their advertising person, or working with their lead person to try to generate more prospects. After our clients have received numerous goodwill calls, they realize the service they are getting is truly "Outrageous," and they often give us referrals on the phone or simply tell others about our service.

By focusing on serving the client as much as on the product we have sold them, we find that they want to buy other products from us as well. We spend so much time with our current clients that we stay busy almost full time selling them additional products and servicing their needs. There is certainly no one better to sell to than an existing client. We would rather have 300 clients with five products each than 1,500 clients with one product each. As we work with these clients on more and more of their needs, the relationship gets closer, and the likelihood of a referral developing gets even greater.

With each referral, another thank-you note goes out and cookies are delivered as a small token of our appreciation. This system of taking care of the customer and responding quickly when the need arises, returning their phone calls promptly, and making the goodwill calls each month develops a close relationship with the customer.

There is nothing magical about what we are doing other than the fact that very few people do it. In my entire business career I have never heard of one single company other than ours that calls their clients each month just to see how they are doing. This could be the most important service we provide, and it gets us new business. If you will simply take care of the customers you have, you will find that they will be bigger customers for you and send you more customers than you can handle. Our agency grows at the rate of our referrals, and that rate has been more than 20 percent per year since the day we started.

CHAPTER

43

You Can Have Everything in Life You Want . . .

Zig Ziglar is my favorite motivational speaker and without question is an inspiration to many salesmen throughout the country. Ziglar says: "You can have everything in life you want if you will just help enough other people get what they want." The problem is that so many people focus on their own wants and desires instead of their customer's wants and desires. The customer sees it; the salesman misses the sale; and both are losers in the end. When I go out on a sales call, I simply visit with the people and find out what it is they want. I sell them the products they want and many times also sell them other products they need as well.

So many times I find sales people stumbling with a customer and not realizing why they can't make a sale. When I go out on a call with them it is absolutely amazing how quickly we get to the bottom line when I just start off the meeting by asking the customer what it is they are looking for. Other salesmen may have spent two or three appointments with the client and gotten nowhere, but by simply asking what they want and then delivering it, a sale can usually be made quickly.

In our business we have all the insurance companies at our disposal, and we have the products clients need. The key is to match their wants and needs with the available products. Ask your clients probing questions to uncover the needs they have and simply deliver the goods. Many salesmen think they can go in and give a good presentation and expect the customer to buy. By asking the right questions and listening very carefully to prospective clients you can help customers get what they want and you can have all you ever wanted in sales.

Fax Information on Your Company Prior to the Appointment

One of the quickest ways to improve your closing ratio is to fax information on your company to your prospect prior to your appointment or call. I have found this technique to work extremely well because it gives information on me and helps clients better understand what we will be presenting. I think all sales people have had the experience of going to see a client for the first time and giving them information on their company along with their company brochure only to have the client glance at the information and set it aside. Once you are actually in the meeting, the prospect will not read the brochure in front of you. When you have finished the presentation, you will leave and the client will likely drop the information you left in a file folder or in the trash and that's the end of it.

I did business this way for quite a while before I decided to fax information on our agency prior to the meeting. If I had several days prior to the appointment I might send a letter. The best combination, however, was to fax the information and follow it up by mailing the original. When the prospect receives the information, they almost feel I am sending them homework or information they need to look over prior to my meeting in order to be prepared for our discussion. They can read the information at a time that is convenient and they will know all about our agency and the "Outrageous Service" we deliver. When I get to the appointment, I am treated totally differently than when they do not get this information prior to my visit.

When I go to a meeting and they have not received this information, I am a total stranger and I do not have any credibility with the client. When they have received our agency brochure and some articles highlighting the "Outrageous Service" our agency provides, I am treated with much more respect. They realize that our agency has been named Arkansas' Business of the Year, that I am one of the top producing health agents in the country, and that our agency stands for "Outrageous Service." They also get a better understanding of the products I will be presenting. It is so noticeable when they have read this information, and often they congratulate me on our accomplishments and tell me how informative the material is. This makes for a totally different meeting and allows me to have instant credibility. They have more trust in me and are much more likely to listen to me about the products we are discussing.

If you really want your clients to read information on your company, then get it to them prior to the appointment and watch your closing ratio go straight up.

The only thing you can take with you when you die is what you gave away while you were living.

Be a Community Volunteer

Why is this chapter under "Outrageous Service Equals Outrageous Sales?" Because by being a community volunteer you are delivering "Outrageous Service" to your community. I currently serve on the Boys Club Board, the Baptist Hospital Health Foundation Board, The American Red Cross Board, and the Arthritis Foundation Board. I coach two YMCA soccer teams and one YMCA basketball team. I also coach and sponsor a men's softball team, and I sponsor several other youth baseball teams. I serve the Little Rock community by being a member of the Little Rock Rotary Club and I am a member of the Second Presbyterian Church. I serve as a frequent motivational speaker to kids' youth groups, to my peers in the insurance field and to other businesses.

All this adds up to a great deal of satisfaction for me, and a lot of sales for our insurance agency. When I am out there working to help other people in a nonprofit capacity the business community rewards me with business. When I go out and coach a young child and help develop a champion's attitude in that child, the parents are eternally grateful. Many of them want to pay me back in some way, and if they ever get a chance to help me business wise, they do so. This is a win/win situation for all involved. I love coaching the kids and developing those lifetime relationships with them, and it is amazing how many of those kids' parents I end up insuring. I will probably insure the kids themselves someday. I have never asked any of my players or nonprofit organizations to let me bid on their insurance plan. When the time comes they call and ask me. If I do a good job in my volunteer work, they can imagine what kind of job I will do for them if I am getting paid for it.

Incidentally, three of the players that I coached years ago in little league football and basketball are now full time employees at our agency. I have hired four former players to work in our agency while they were attending college. The friendships that have turned into business relationships from these volunteer activities are too numerous to count.

Every community needs business people to be volunteers, and volunteers will always be in high demand. By going out and helping others, you will be rewarded because what goes around always comes around.

CHAPTER

Become the Best at What You Do and You Will Never Have to Prospect Again

When I started The Hatcher Agency on September 1, 1990, I made calls to everybody I knew to let them know I was in business. I did this for the first three months, and after each call I sent the prospect information on our agency. I listed in my database the people who asked me to get in touch with them at a later date. In those three months I generated so much activity that I have never made a cold call since. I get all my business today by referral. Although there are agents in our office who make some prospect calls, I always tell them if they are doing enough good things for their current customers, they will never have to pick up the telephone again.

I do not know if I would ever be able to return to calling people and have them treat me like an insurance salesman. Many times they would hang up on me or brush me off and tell me they were too busy or did not want to hear the sales pitch I tried to squeeze in before they lost interest. Actually, in those first three months, I did not try to make a sales pitch as much as I just tried to tell people what I was doing and ask for the opportunity to bid on any of their programs.

I find the best sales approach is simply to try to let people know what you do and help them get what they want. Once you get an opportunity to help them, you must do your job so well that they and everyone else will want to purchase from you. I have never seen the best surgeon at a loss for business, nor have I seen the very best baseball player in need of a team to play on. If you focus on becoming the best in your business, you will never need to make prospect calls; and you will have more business than you can handle.

The key is to make the commitment to do the little things every day that give your customers the very best service and to commit to do the training and continuing education necessary to become the best in your profession. Success is very simple. The key question is: "Who has the discipline to do the things to make themselves the best?" For me, it is easier to pay the price to become the best at what I do than it is to have to prospect and convince people to try to give me an open ear. If you will implement these concepts and principles, I think you will enjoy doing your business almost exclusively by referral as I have.

Cross Training

At The Hatcher Agency we believe in the concept of cross training. When we do our training sessions each week, the secretary, the service representatives, the office manager and the salesmen are all present. We want each person to know everything there is to know about the other person's job so we do our training on all positions with all people present. This is why our training is scheduled for 7:00 a.m. to 8:00 a.m. before the business day gets started. That way, we are able to train and still are available for our customers. If a call comes in during training, we send the person out that needs to handle that call and proceed with the rest of our group.

I heard Tom Peters say once that Embassy Suites was famous for cross training their employees. They thought it was important that the maid also knew how to be a cook and vice versa. If they were running short on cooks one day, they could bring in a maid who was cross-trained, and she could help out in the kitchen. They also found that the maid could highly recommend the hotel's pancakes to their customers because she had first-hand experience making them. This led to more business in their kitchen because if the entire hotel staff is on board with what is going on in the kitchen, they will sell more business for the restaurant.

At The Hatcher Agency it is important that we all understand each other's job just as five players on a basketball court each need to understand the other's position. This cross training not only allows us to promote people from within when new positions open up, but also allows us to have a person fill in for another should we need extra help in a pinch. So many companies take the attitude that the employee is going to learn his job and his job only and not worry about the other departments in the company. How can you develop the best possible winning team if you have a bunch of different units that do not understand how all the pieces work together? If everyone understands how the others operate, you can all move in one direction toward the common goal. Cross training is a necessity for any champion organization.

PART FIVE

Outrageous Education and Training

> *Treating my employees well makes me
> feel better as well as my employees.*

Fringe and Intangible Benefits Can Lower Turnover and Improve Service

In a previous chapter, we talked about paying employees a little more to get the very best. In addition to pay, there are other fringe and intangible benefits you can provide employees that can make as much difference as their salaries. When you put the two together, you can really lower the turnover in your organization and get happier and more productive employees.

At The Hatcher Agency we have no cubicles. Every employee has a private office. It is unrealistic to think that every employer in America can eliminate cubicles in its office complex. However, in a personal service organization like ours, it is possible. The office building we purchased was previously a dentist's office that had 40 patient rooms. Needless to say these rooms were not big, but they all had doors and provided private space for each employee. When we purchased the building, it had been vacant for three years, and we totally remodeled the inside. Each office has its own computer, a nice workstation and, most importantly, a door. One of our big selling points to prospective employees is that everybody will have a private office. Each office has a picture on the wall and a comfortable chair and is a pleasant place to work. Employees spend over 50 percent of their waking hours in these offices. I want this to be a pleasant experience for them and for me since I spend more time in my office than in my home.

We also provide at the company's expense full coverage for health, dental, life insurance, short term disability, long term disability, long term care, vision care and a 401(K) retirement plan for each employee. We do not pay for family health insurance coverage, but provide this as an option that the employee can have payroll deducted through a pre-tax Section 125 Cafeteria Plan. We also offer our employees the option of enrolling in a voluntary cancer plan and a voluntary supplemental group life plan.

I always tell our clients and employees that you do not have to be a big company to have great benefits, you simply have to be a company that wants to provide great benefits. Our benefit package is as good as that of any client we insure and is something I am very proud of. By paying for these benefits for employees, we let them know that we care about them and that they are working for a first-class organization that wants to have first-class people. Employee benefits are a tax-deductible expense to the employer, and they are a tax-free benefit to the employee. Fringe benefits are a better bang for our buck because we can pass on benefits to the employee that he would be taxed on if he bought them individually. In addition, coverage such as dental, vision, long term care, short term disability and long term disability are almost impossible to purchase on an individual policy basis; and if we did not provide the coverage, our employees probably would not have coverage.

Another reason for providing these benefits is that the last thing I want to happen is to have an employee who needs dental work done but cannot afford it. Also, I do not want an employee who cannot get eye-glasses for the children because he or she cannot afford it. Or worst of all, have an employee who cannot get health care for a family member that is ill. If our employees could not get the health care they need or were not able to retire after working here for 40 years, that would send a message that this is not a company that can be counted on.

Although our benefit package is a rich one, our company is probably tougher than others are when it comes to personal days off. Employees have ten personal days a year that they can use for sickness or vacation, to attend a funeral, or to take care of personal business. After working for other companies early in my career and watching employees skip work by taking sick days and abusing the sick pay and personal leave policies, I decided I really did not care why an employee was off. If they are off, they are not there to serve our customers.

Rather than decide how many sick days and vacation days employees need and evaluate whether they are abusing the system, I implemented ten personal days for all first year employees, and increase the personal days as their tenure increases. This gives the employee the incentive to make the best use of these ten days. I have found that this incentive works very well and that employees obviously do not want to fake a sick day when they can simply take a vacation day. They are more likely to schedule the children's doctor appointments and their own appointments at the end of the day rather than miss an entire workday. By setting up these personal days with proper incentives, our clients actually get better service because our employees are predictable and are at work to serve them.

Let's look at an example of how important personal days can be to your company. Let's say you give your employees five sick days and five vacation days per year. One employee takes the five vacation days, but shows up for work the rest of the year and does not utilize the five sick days. This employee is very productive for you but only gets five days off during the year. Another employee takes the five vacation days and is not sick, but because the five sick days are available, calls in sick five times during the year. The attitude is "Hey, I'm going to take the sick days that are in my contract and get the days off that I deserve."

Employees who take sick days because they "have them coming" cause all kinds of problems. First of all, since they cannot schedule sick days ahead of time, they have to call in each morning to report that they will not be at work that day. They couldn't plan ahead and tell another employee what things needed to be done, so the work they needed to do that day is left unfinished. Secondly, employees are forced to lie in order to take all their sick days, and that does not make them feel good. In most cases other employees of the company also know when someone is playing hooky, and this promotes a bad environment for good customer service. If employees have ten personal days instead of five vacation days and five sick days, they only call in when they are truly sick. If they want to take a day off to do some personal things, they will get their work finished before they take off and tell their clients that they will not be there the next day so everybody can plan around it.

I cannot say how frustrating it would be to have a big day ahead of me and need a lot of proposals typed only to have the secretary call in and say she was sick, especially when I realized she was "taking her sick days" before the end of the year. This would be unproductive for our company and for me. It is important to provide incentives for employees to get to work so they can provide great service.

49

Yes, We Have a
Full-Time Trainer

I read in a Tom Peters book that cross training employees was one of the most valuable things a company could ever do for itself. Many business owners are afraid to train their employees because they fear employees will take this important training and go to work for the competition. As Tom Peters says, "You have two choices. You can train your employees, or you can have an untrained workforce. Which is worse?"

We are a relatively small company of only 23 employees. Still, if I had to sit down with every new employee and take time to train them on all the facets of our company, or if I had to take another employee off the job to do it, it would reduce our customer service substantially. This would be stressful for employees who were pulled off their jobs to conduct training, and it would make new employees feel rushed and unable to get the type training they need. How do I know all of this? For the first four years our company operated without a trainer.

I finally decided that turnover was a part of business, and although I tried to keep our turnover as low as possible, we hired new employees due to our constant growth and the fact that we did have people leave. I chose one of our most competent employees who is a former school-teacher and made her our trainer. When new employees are hired, she teaches them how our computer system works and is available for consultation the first two to three months of their employment. She travels with them to appointments to keep them from making big mistakes, and she trains them on the day to day details involved with our company. Our trainer is a licensed insurance agent who understands the entire gamut of our company and is an invaluable asset to our company. The person you hire as your trainer needs to be a person who has already worked for the company and understands the message that you want new employees to hear. Good trainers will set the tone for your business because they are the ones that teach the new service professionals for your company.

Another benefit we have received from our full time trainer is that she can do special projects for us when there are no new employees to train. When we have an employee out sick or on vacation, she immediately jumps into that job so customer service is not interrupted. By filling in for other employees, she stays current on what is going on in the field so she can better train new employees.

With a work force of 23 employees you can pretty well count on having a new employee to train, someone out of the office or a special project that needs to be done. Our trainer never has down time. We never feel we are wasting money on the position because there is always something to do.

For a larger company, multiple trainers or several replacement employees may be necessary. As our company grows we will certainly have additional trainers or cross-trained employees who have no job other than to fill in for people who are out. Having employees out of the office is part of business, but having a trained person replace the person who is out can help your company deliver service superior to your competitor, or, should I say "Outrageous Service."

CHAPTER

50

All Employees go to Insurance School

At The Hatcher Agency we require everybody, including secretaries, to go to insurance school. A lot of people might ask why in the world a secretary needs to get an insurance agent's license and go through an insurance school and exam? The answer is simple: it makes the employee more knowledgeable.

We like the fact that all employees are told during the interview process that they must go to insurance school and pass the exam in order to keep their job with us. Although it may scare off some people, they are generally the ones we want to scare off. It is a requirement, a standard that all of our employees must meet, and our employees take pride in having passed the exam and in knowing that all employees at The Hatcher Agency will be educated winners. When I am interviewing an employee, I do not tell them they have to pass the exam on the first try; I just let them know that they will be taking the exam until they pass. If an employee has not passed by the third time, we require them to pay for their own exams. This generally gets their attention; they study a little harder and pass. We have never had an employee that did not eventually pass the exam, but we have had a few employees that have had to study extra hard and extra long in order to meet this goal.

Taking the insurance exam is our first step toward continuing education for all of our employees. In any industry, training and education are what separates the best from their competitors. Having intelligent, well-trained people and sending them to seminars, motivational talks and trade schools is important for all employees. After all, you spend so much money on their salaries and benefits, it just makes sense to spend a few extra dollars a year to hone their skills.

All people enjoy learning. Some employees may be afraid of training and resist it; but when we learn, it puts a smile on our face and makes us feel better about ourselves. If employees feel good about themselves and are well educated, they are going to give your customers even better service.

My advice is to set a standard in your organization for all of your employees and have a ladder of continuing education for your employees to climb. And, as Zig Ziglar says, "We will see you at the top!"

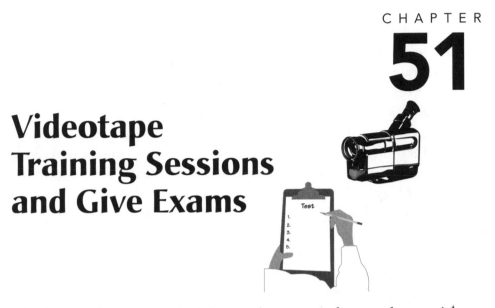

Videotape Training Sessions and Give Exams

We always videotape our training sessions so employees who are sick or out on an appointment can watch the training session. That way, we don't have to teach it over and over. These training tapes are also extremely helpful when we hire new employees because they can watch a videotaped series and we don't have to spend valuable time redoing the training for each new person.

We give each employee an exam following the training sessions. Before I do a session, I dictate the exam and have the secretary type it. Then I make sure all the answers to the test questions are in the videotape by using the exam as an outline.

The exam is not designed to intimidate employees or to make them feel badly if they don't get a great score. The purpose is to let employees know they will be held accountable to know the information. That motivates them to pay more attention to the videotapes. All employees continue watching the videotape and retaking the exam until they score 100 percent. We do not believe in 70, 80 or even 90 percent on our exam. How would you like it if a heart surgeon only had to score 70 percent on his procedures? You would not feel very good about having that person do heart surgery on you. When we are servicing the customer, we need to be 100 percent.

In order to develop exams for your company, all you have to do is dictate questions on the area you want to do training in. The key to good training sessions is to take one particular item that you want all employees in your company to know, focus on that item, and include in the session every single detail your employees need to know.

For example, if you owned a Waffle House, you might do a videotaped training session on how to cook a waffle. It may sound like a pretty simple procedure, but when you try to teach people in thousands of Waffle Houses throughout the country how to make a waffle exactly the same way, it is not simple. Your training session might include how to make the batter, what the temperature of the waffle iron should be before putting the batter in it, how long it takes to cook a waffle, how to add blueberries to your waffle, and on and on.

Great organizations take care of the details by training their employees to do their very best. No matter how simple your business is, it always becomes complicated when you start getting a lot of customers for one little product. Training is the only way to get it done. One of our clients is TCBY, the famous yogurt company. This appears to be a fairly simple business. After all, they sell yogurt with a few toppings on it. However, it isn't as easy as it seems. TCBY brings managers and employees to their training site to teach them how to make sundaes, shivers, shakes, and waffle cones. Each employee goes through extensive training, and that is what sets TCBY apart from the majority of their competitors. They train their store managers, franchise owners and hourly employees to make sure that each person has the very best knowledge and training when they go to their job. Training is what made TCBY a great company and keeps them a great company. They call their training "Yogurt U" (for "Yogurt University).

If you want to be the best, a company training program is essential.

> *A good education is something*
> *you never finish.*

Read a Book a Month

I remember thinking when I graduated from college, thank God I am through with school at last. Boy, was I wrong! I quickly learned that if you are going to be successful in life, education is something you start in kindergarten and do not finish until the day you die. If you think you are through with school because you graduated and passed that licensing exam you will soon find out how wrong you are.

In his seminars Zig Ziglar says that motivation is not permanent, but then again, neither is bathing. This bit of humor makes the point that you cannot come to a Zig Ziglar seminar, listen to his talks, and be motivated for the rest of your life. You must continue to listen to his tapes, read his books, and continue to keep good thoughts going into your brain in order to stay motivated and achieve peak performance. Zig says that you cannot take a bath one time and be clean for the rest of your life. However, it is amazing how many people give up trying to improve their education once they are through with school and employed. We all get caught up in the hustle and bustle of raising our children, keeping a spouse happy, trying to stay in good shape, and trying to get our jobs done; and we forget about continuing our education.

A friend told me that accomplishing new things is a cinch by the inch, but quite hard by the yard. My father exemplifies this principle more than anyone else I know. He has always pointed out that doing a little bit on a steady basis each and every day is much more productive than doing something obsessively for short periods of time.

One of my education goals is to read a book a month for the rest of my life. I implemented this goal a couple of years ago and I find that I generally read two or three books a month. This means that when the year is over, I have more than met my goal. The choice of books is very important. I tend to choose books that will broaden my education, help my business, keep me motivated or add new insights regarding better ways to take care of our customers. These books also improve some area of my personal life, which, of course, is the most important.

Some books I have read recently and highly recommend include:

1. *I'll See You at the Top* by Zig Ziglar
2. *Success is a Choice* by Rick Pitino
3. *Management Methods Of Jesus* by Bob Briner
4. *Tuesdays with Morrie* by Mitch Albom
5. *Don't Sweat the Small Stuff (and It's All Small Stuff)* by Richard Carlson
6. *How To Double Your Profits in Six Months* by Bob Fifer
7. *The Complete Idiots Guide to Getting Rich* by Larry Waschka
8. *Don't Worry, Make Money* by Richard Carlson
9. *Don't Sweat the Small Stuff with Your Family* by Richard Carlson
10. *Seven Habits of Highly Effective People* by Stephen Covey
11. *In Search of Excellence* by Tom Peters
12. *The Beginner's Bible* as told by Karyn Henley
13. *The Feldman Method* by Ben Feldman
14. *The Partner* by John Grisham

15. *Bits and Pieces* (Monthly Motivational Booklet) by The Economics Press, Inc., 12 Daniel Road, Fairfield, NJ 07004-2565
16. *Simplify Your Life* by Elaine St. James
17. *Over the Top* by Zig Ziglar
18. *They Call Me Coach* by John Wooden
19. *The Road Less Traveled* by M. Scott Peck, M.D.
20. *Eat To Win* by Robert Haas
21. *Made in America: My Story* by Sam Walton

These are some of my all time favorites and some that I have read recently that I think you will enjoy. I also read the local newspaper, trade magazines, and *Sports Illustrated* each week. Believe it or not, *Sports Illustrated* helps me more in business than it gives me pleasure. Reading about the sacrifices of the very best athletes in the world helps me better see the price I must pay in business to be a success. Likewise, when I read about the mistakes that some of these athletes make, it serves as a reminder that success can be fleeting if you don't operate with integrity and good character.

Reading a book a month will improve your vocabulary, make you a more well rounded individual and give you some quiet time for reflection, which all of us need. I have received so many good thoughts from books that I can't even begin to tell you how important they have been for our business. At all our weekly staff meetings I read a chapter from *Don't Sweat the Small Stuff and It's All Small Stuff* to my staff. This book is a summary of ideas with brief chapters that can be read quickly and make a very important point for our staff to ponder for the day. Reading a book a month will improve your education as well as your business results.

CHAPTER

53

Speaker of the Month

Each month at The Hatcher Agency we bring in a speaker to talk to all our employees. This speaker is generally someone from another field outside the insurance industry. I try to find the very best people in other lines of business and have them come in and tell our staff what it is they do that makes them successful. Professionals that have come to speak to our group have included the top bond salesman, the top business forms salesman, the top oncologist, the top football coach, the top financial planner, the top stockbroker, and the top car salesman in the area.

What our employees love about this is that they get to hear from somebody who has been in the trenches what makes a person success-ful. We all learn from their talks—and believe it or not—the speakers actually get a lot out of it. We do not pay these speakers, but we gener-ally give them a $50 gift certificate to a restaurant—or, if we know a particular passion they have, we may get them a gift that will help them pursue their passion. I always offer to return the favor for them and their organization at any time, and often do.

It is important to bring in these speakers each month as all employees in any organization need a boost from time to time, and ours need to hear it from someone other than me. The interesting thing is that many times the speakers say so many of the things we teach in training, and that just drives deeper the principles we are trying to instill. We generally have our speaker of the month come late on a Friday afternoon and serve cookies and soft drinks. Then we send the employees off for a productive weekend with plenty of time for creative thinking so they can come into the next week fully charged. When you use speakers from the local area, you honor them, and you also expose your employees to their services. Everyone likes to be recognized as the best in their profession, and you can give them that recognition and provide a valuable service to your staff at a very low cost.

For larger companies, it is a good idea to bring in professional speakers such as Zig Ziglar, Tom Hopkins, Tom Peters and Lou Holtz, among others, to keep your employees consistently motivated. Video tapes, cassettes, books and other training materials from these valuable speakers can help give your troops the right attitude that is necessary to succeed in business.

Zig Ziglar says bathing is not permanent; and neither is motivation. It is something that obviously needs to be done on an ongoing basis.

Some Final Thoughts

Don't Be
Afraid to Fail

One of the most amazing things to me is how many people will not try something new because they are afraid they will fail. It happens to all of us at a very early age. I have a nine-year-old daughter, five-year-old twin girls, and a seven-month-old son. I spend a lot of time at the lake teaching my kids and their friends to ski. It always surprises me that many of these five-to-nine-year-old girls are afraid to even try to learn to water ski. It is not so much that they are afraid of the water; they are afraid they cannot ski. This is especially true if there are other children present who have tried and succeeded at getting up on the skis. These children won't try because they are afraid they will fail.

"We are born to win, but as soon as we get out of the womb, society conditions us to fail." By age five, many children are already learning the fear of failure. Their parents have not encouraged them to try new things because the parents have their own fears, and they don't want to see the children fail. When my children say, "I can't," I tell them those words are simply not acceptable. The only words I will accept are, "I'll try." I want to instill in my children at a very early age that failure is ok, but refusing to try is unacceptable.

One of my all-time favorite poems is called "The Race." The first time I read the poem I almost cried. It is a poem about a young child with courage and the will to continue to try and a father in the stands who rewards him for his ability to get up and try again. We all need to realize that there is nothing to lose by trying. If we try and fail, we are no worse off than if we had not tried to begin with. Actually, if we do not try, we may be worse off because we may begin a practice that could become a habit and a way of life.

More than anything else, attitude determines the success a person will have in life. Top salespeople in any profession always have a wonderful attitude. You simply cannot be a top salesperson year in and year out with a poor attitude. You have to be willing to try new things, to continue to learn, to implement new concepts and to be open to new ideas. If you are not willing to try new things, you will simply be passed by.

The older we get, the more we tend to be afraid of failure. The reason is that we add to our list of failures each year. As those failures add up, we become more resistant to trying new things, as we almost would rather not succeed than to take the chance of trying and failing one more time.

If you study the lives of the greatest people in this world, you will be amazed at all the failures they have had. The common denominator for all these people who have had so many failures is that they have gotten out there and tried again. We all know that Michael Jordan was cut from his high school basketball team but went on to become the greatest basketball player of all time. Many other people in sports have failed miserably many times before they became a huge success.

One of the most amazing records of failure is the one listed below.

Failed in business	age 22
Ran for legislature (defeated)	age 23
Failed in business	age 24
Elected to legislature	age 25
Sweetheart died	age 26
Had a nervous breakdown	age 27
Defeated for speaker	age 29
Defeated for elector	age 31
Defeated for Congress	age 34
Elected to Congress	age 37
Defeated for Congress	age 39
Defeated for Senate	age 46
Defeated for Vice President	age 47
Defeated for Senate	age 49
Elected President of the United States	age 51

That is the record of Abraham Lincoln. Obviously, Abraham Lincoln had a heck of a lot more failures than successes, but overall he was a huge success because of his courage, persistence and perseverance.

My father has always kidded me that I have one of the most selective memories of any person he has ever known. He says I always seem to remember only the accomplishments of my high school and college sports careers and in my business dealings and forget many of the difficult times I had over the years. He says when I recall the past, all I remember is the good.

I am not sure that my having a selective memory is so bad. Who knows? This "selective memory" may be what gives me the ability to go forward and to try virtually any new challenge. Because I remember my successes and focus on them, I have the confidence to believe that I can do just about anything. I have successfully tried many things just for the sake of knowing that I have attempted and completed them. When I accomplish a new task, it gives me more confidence to take on the next challenge.

Some examples of challenges that I have attempted and accomplished include: running a marathon, completing a triathlon, completing a 150-mile bike race, sky diving, para-sailing, scuba diving, taking over 2,000 hours in continuing education at insurance schools and passing more than 40 insurance exams, writing this book, starting my own business, and making the starting lineup on three different college sports teams after beginning as a walk-on. I have called back to insurance companies who rejected me earlier to develop a better relationship; and I have gone back to try to mend differences with vendors, friends and competitors with whom I had differences.

I get along with all types of people and have friends from all walks of life, but my very best friends are people who are willing to try new things and are not afraid to fail. I want to spend my time with people who continue to grow, and to grow you must be willing to try new things.

Following you will find some of my favorite motivational poems. I hope they inspire you and you like them as much as I do.

The Guy in the Glass

When you get what you want in your struggle for pelf,
And the world makes you King for a day,
Then go to the mirror and look at yourself,
And see what that guy has to say.
For it isn't your Father, or Mother, or Wife
Who judgement upon you must pass.
The feller whose verdict counts most in your life,
Is the guy staring back from the glass.
He's the feller to please, never mind all the rest,
For he's with you clear up to the end,
And you've passed your most dangerous, difficult test
If the guy in the glass is your friend.
You may be like Jack Horner and "chisel" a plum
And think you're a wonderful guy,

But the man in the glass says you're only a bum
If you can't look him straight in the eye.
You can fool the whole world down the pathway of years,
And get pats on your back as you pass.
But your final reward will be heartaches and tears
If you've cheated the guy in the glass.

—Dale Wimbrow

It's all in a State of Mind

If you think you are beaten, you are;
If you think you dare not, you won't.
If you like to win, but don't think you can,
It's almost a cinch you won't.

If you think you'll lose, you've lost;
For out in the world you'll find
Success begins with a fellow's will;
It's all in a state of mind.

For many a game is lost
Before even a play is run,
And many a coward fails
Before even his work has begun.

Think big and your deeds will grow,
Think small and you'll fall behind,
Think that you can and you will;
It's all in a state of mind.

If you think you are outclassed you are;
You've got to think high to rise;
You've got to be sure of yourself before
You can ever take home the prize.

Life's battles don't always go
To the stronger or faster man,
More often than not, the man who wins
Is the fellow who thinks he can.

—AUTHOR UNKNOWN

*In major league baseball they spend a
lot of time reporting how many home
runs somebody hits in a season, but
they spend hardly any time reporting
how many times a player strikes out.*

Swing for the Fences

When I was in my senior year at Alma College in Michigan, Hall of
Famer Willie Stargel came to speak to our Fellowship of Christian
Athletes. Stargel was the captain and Most Valuable Player for the
Pittsburgh Pirates who won the 1979 World Series. Willie gave an
hour talk, and I will never forget the way he ended his speech.

He said he had been asked many times what was the greatest thing
he learned during his career as a professional baseball player. Willie
said the answer was very clear. "In the early years of my major league
career when I came up to the plate with the bases loaded and two outs,
I would say to myself, 'Please Lord, don't let me strike out. Let me make
contact with the ball because the last thing I want to do is strike out
with the bases loaded.'" Willie said he did not strike out much early in
his career. He often hit a ground ball to the second baseman or a fly ball
to the right fielder that ended the inning with no runs scored, but he
didn't strike out.

Later in his career, when Willie came up to bat with the bases loaded and two outs, he learned to swing to hit the ball as hard as he could and knock it out of the ballpark. He said he struck out a heck of a lot more than he did early in his career. However, he also hit quite a few grand slams and a whole lot of doubles and singles as well. He became the hero for the Pittsburgh Pirates many times by swinging as hard as he could in a critical situation. He finally realized that whether he struck out trying to hit the ball out of the park or hit a ground ball to the second baseman, the result was an out. Early in his career, Willie spent his at-bat trying not to fail. Later in his career, when he was no longer afraid to strike out, he came to the plate and swung as hard as he could to help his team win.

When you go out in the business world tomorrow and in your everyday life, there will be times when you feel like Willie Stargel coming to bat with the bases loaded and two outs. When you get in the batter's box and you feel that fear, step out of the box for a second; adjust your attitude; step back in the box; and swing for the fences. When you do, you will feel better about yourself, and you will often be a hero like Willie Stargel. You can never be the hero if you don't take a big swing. Good luck, and swing for the fences!